IT WASN'T MEANT TO BE EASY

IT WASN'T MEANT TO BE EASY

Tamie Fraser in Canberra

CHRISTINA HINDHAUGH

LOTHIAN PUBLISHING COMPANY

MELBOURNE·SYDNEY·AUCKLAND

First published 1986
by Lothian Publishing Company Pty Ltd
Produced by Ross Publishing

Hindhaugh, Christina, 1944-   .
   It wasn't meant to be easy.

   ISBN 0 85091 264 4.

   1. Fraser, Malcolm, 1930-   . 2. Fraser, Tamie
   (Tamara). 3. Prime ministers – Australia. 4. Prime
   ministers' wives – Australia – Biography. 5. Australia
   – Politics and government – 1976-   . I. Title.

994.06'3

Designed by Sandra Nobes
Typeset by Meredith Typesetting
Printed by Globe Press

Photographs supplied by *The Age*, Australian News and Information Bureau, Australian Women's Weekly

CONTENTS

INTRODUCTION

Writing a book about your big sister wasn't meant to be easy—but it was a great adventure! During many hours of interviewing both here and at Nareen Tam swept me along on a colourful journey of exploration and re-discovery into her years at The Lodge. Mostly in peals of laughter, sometimes hotly indignant, occasionally in tears on each other's shoulders, re-living that period has been a remarkable experience for us.

Before I began, someone said: 'Ah, but will the book reveal the real Tamie Fraser?' I hope so. As David Barnett, Malcolm's former press secretary and now writer for *The Bulletin* pointed out: 'The significant thing about your sister was that she was a woman of great character and strength—which she always sought to hide.

'Her public image of a flighty, chatty, ever-so-nice decorative lady was never what she really was, and something she never could have been to have survived as a PM's wife, or as Malcolm Fraser's wife.

'She was actually a person of great toughness and strength—and it'd be a shame if you don't get something of that into the book.' David, I think it's here—and more besides—if only people look beneath the surface of her self-effacing tales.

The book is structured in a rather quaint way, with extensive use of the first person, because the manner in which Tam speaks is so much a feature of her personality, that I wanted readers to hear as much of her story as possible in her own words.

Many people supported me in the writing of this book, and I am grateful to them all; first and foremost, Tam herself; then Malcolm, who, although away in South Africa for much of the time of writing, contributed freely whenever he was home; plus the Fraser children—for all their help and support.

As well, I would like to thank my other sister, Eda Ritchie, my brother, Hugh Beggs, and Tam's three secretaries—Susannah Clarke, Amanda Derham, and Caroline Sande—all of whom gave so generously of their time and enthusiasm; plus Margaret Kelly, Dale Budd, David Barnett, Alastair Drysdale, Judy Baillieu, Dimity Davy, Dinny Killen, Margot Anthony, Edwina Bunny, Jannee Grambeau, Jill Lewis, and a special thank you to Patricia White.

Finally, I want to pay tribute to my husband, Christopher, without whose constant help and encouragement this book never would have been written; and to my children, Julia, Eda and James, without whose constant help and encouragement it may have been written in half the time.

Christina (Petee) Hindhaugh
Balmoral, 1986

vii

For our parents

Chapter 1
NOVEMBER 11

'When a woman's world is falling apart around her ears and she remains inwardly calm and serene,' wrote American poet Judith Viorst, 'chances are her hair is looking fabulous.'

Tamie Fraser's hair needed to look fabulous on the day of November 11, 1975, and as fate or whatever would have it she was actually at the hairdresser in South Yarra, Melbourne, when she first heard the news that rocked a nation.

'Gough's been sacked,' said Malcolm, ringing her there—first and immediately, as always. 'Can you come up?' Tamie left the salon and drove straight back to their Melbourne home in nearby Fairlie Court to pack. She had no great sense of excitement or anticipation, just a feeling of overwhelming relief that the terrible strain of the last four weeks was over.

'We knew things couldn't go on,' she told me later. 'Malcolm had come home from Canberra the weekend before and said: "something has to be done. Kerr will have to make a decision. The country can't be left in a mess like this over Christmas." '

Unlike the rest of Australia on that November afternoon, Tamie had no idea that Malcolm had been appointed caretaker Prime Minister. The possibility had never occurred to her. She arrived back at Fairlie Court and found her son Mark, aged 17, standing at the front door, a bewildered expression on his face. He was at home studying for HSC exams. 'What on earth's going on?' he said. 'Everyone's saying Dad's the PM.'

'Nonsense, darling,' said Tam. 'But Gough's been sacked, thank God, and now there'll be an election. At last the nightmare's over.' But in many ways the nightmare was only beginning, and it was to last for nearly seven and a half years.

Few mothers can drop everything and just walk out—however momentous the occasion. Besides, Tamie wanted to talk to the children before she left. At that time the two boys and Phoebe were day students at nearby Melbourne Grammar and Angela was a boarder. The afternoon disappeared in a rush of re-arranging after-school activities, packing lunches, organising evening meals and leaving enough clean clothes to last the family until she returned. And of course the telephone never stopped ringing.

She was finally able to get away about five, when Christina Hay arrived back at the house. Christina was living with the Fraser family at Fairlie Court at that time to be with the children in the evenings and generally lend a hand when Tamie and Malcolm were away. During the day she worked in the city and that afternoon had come home as soon as she could, knowing she would be needed—and all aglow with the news.

'Let me tell you how I heard about it!', she said, in a phrase Tam was to hear a thousand times over in the years to come. 'I was in a crowded tram in the city just after lunch and an old derelict got on and yelled: "Gough's been sacked! He's got the boot!" and no-one took the slightest notice except for one man down the front who told him to sit down and shutup. Then three stops later a ticket inspector got on board and said: "Hey! I just can't keep this to myself!" and announced the news, and the whole tram erupted.'

*   *   *   *   *

Of course everyone can remember what they were doing on November 11, 1975, the moment they first heard the news of Gough Whitlam's dismissal by the

Governor-General, Sir John Kerr. The momentous event had occurred after months of tension over various allegations of financial mismanagement and, finally, refusal of supply by the opposition dominated Senate. Gough Whitlam's intention of carrying on without supply brought the matter to a climax.

I wish I could record here that I was wind-surfing off the Great Barrier Reef, abseiling in the Grampians or at least chairing a high level executive conference in Melbourne. But in fact I was at home, in the kitchen.

I live on a property near a small town called Balmoral in the redgum country of south-western Victoria not far from the Frasers' home at Nareen, and during the years that followed when my sister Tamie was buzzing frenetically around Canberra, Australia, and indeed the world, I was mostly at home and often in the kitchen.

On the surface our lives could not have been more separate. But the telephone is a powerful link for people who know each other well. It imparts so much more than words. The tone of the voice, its timbre, its pauses and inflections, its sighs and chuckles—in the hands of ardent and dedicated exponents like us, the telephone can reveal as much as a face to face conversation, maybe more. So although for much of the seven and a half years we were all far apart, Tamie remained in constant touch with her family.

Which is not to say she ever told us what was really going on, and the news of Sir John Kerr's action bowled us over. I was stunned, knocked sideways. I had never thought through such a possibility and so when it happened I found it too dramatic to absorb, too monumental to contain. I bundled our three small children into the farm ute and drove off across the property until I reached the paddock where my husband was driving on his tractor in ever-diminishing circles, cutting hay. He was coming up out of a gully when I first caught sight of him, still driving flat out but standing straight upright, like a soldier, at the wheel of his tractor, his radio earphones still on his head. 'I felt I just had to make some kind of gesture to the occasion,' he said by way of explanation. It was a feeling mirrored right across the nation.

Eda Ritchie, my other sister, was doing the household shopping in a nearby country town on that November afternoon. She was loading some parcels into her car when up rushed the local postmaster, red in the face and shaking with rage. 'Kerr's sacked Whitlam!' he gasped. 'Sacked 'im, and put that bastard Fraser in his place!' Too breathless with fury to continue he stood in the middle of the pavement and shook both fists high in the air. That too was a gesture to the occasion.

Meanwhile Dad and my brother Hugh Beggs were busy classing stud rams in the sheep yards outside the woolshed at Nareeb Nareeb, bending over the race to examine and assess each animal as it came past and then draft it off into pens of different grades. They had several men helping them. The woolshed door opened behind them and someone shouted the news. All work ceased abruptly, and for a moment there was a stunned silence.

Then one of the station hands said: 'Well, I like him.'

'Who?' everyone cried at once. 'Whitlam? Kerr? Fraser?'

'No, this ram,' he replied, and bending over the sheep went back to work once more. That too, in its own way, was a gesture to the occasion.

The moment Tam's aircraft touched down in Canberra she was whisked away in a Commonwealth car to where Malcolm was waiting to see her. After all those weeks of shared tension and trial, what did she say to him? What did he say to her? I do not know. There are some things even a sister doesn't ask.

But I do know they dined at the Commonwealth Club that night with a few friends. It was no great celebration. Everyone just sagged with relief that at last a decision had been made and an election called.

On the way back to their hotel after dinner Tamie noticed a flag on the front of their car and suddenly realised they were riding in the Prime Ministerial car.

'I don't think this is right,' she said to Malcolm. 'I don't feel comfortable about it. After all, you're only the caretaker PM.'

'I know, I don't like it either, love,' said Malcolm. 'But it's necessary. It's the position that's important. The position must be protected through continuity.' She sighed and nodded. She could see his point but was never happy with the trappings of Prime Minister until they had been truly won at the ballot box. Towards midnight they arrived at the Canberra Rex hotel where Malcolm had been staying, and were hustled inside through a kitchen door right at the back of the building.

'The place was crawling with security officers,' Tamie told me later. 'We were taken down a long dark passageway, then up in the service lift, then along another endless corridor all lined with security people—to our bedroom. And when we got inside I said to Malcolm, "I can't believe it! It's hideous! Is this the freedom we've been fighting for?" And suddenly it hit her, the awful realisation that all this would be part of their lives from now on, certainly up until the election, and possibly beyond.

Chapter 2
CAMPAIGN TRAIL

The 1975 Liberal election campaign got away to a shaky start—literally. A few days before the launch the Frasers attended a Liberal Party function at the Penshurst race course in western Victoria, and received a rousing welcome from the large crowd. It was a mild, sunny day and most of the men were in shirt sleeves while the women were wearing summer dresses.

The caretaker Prime Minister circulated through the crowd wearing a long-sleeved shirt, two jumpers, a sports coat, and a heavy overcoat over the top. And even then he couldn't stop shivering.

By that evening he was back at Fairlie Court in bed, running a high fever and sweating like Niagara Falls. Journalists came in flocks and hovered around the house, constantly ringing the front door bell and asking: 'How is the Prime Minister feeling?'

'Have you ever had the 'flu?' said Tamie. 'Then *that's* how he's feeling!'

Next morning the telephone went at 6am. It was another zealous journalist. 'I believe the Prime Minister is carrying on the affairs of state from his bedside?' he said.

'No, he's not!' Tamie snapped. 'He's sound asleep!'

'Oh,' said the journalist, clearly disappointed.

'It's six o'clock in the morning, for God's sake!' said Tamie. '*It's six o'clock in the morning!*' It was not the last time she was to find the press intruding into their private lives.

Mr. Whitlam launched the Labor Party's election campaign at a lunch time rally in Sydney's Domain Park on Monday, November 24, and delivered his televised policy speech that evening from Melbourne's Festival Hall. While the capacity crowd chanted 'We want Gough! We want Gough!' Mr. Whitlam appealed to voters to restore the mandate which he said had been stolen from him, and stressed that Bill Hayden (his Treasurer's) recent budget was the only way to restore the nation's prosperity and should be given a go. Malcolm lay in his sick bed, churning with indignation, and watched the speech on television.

The Liberal Party campaign was to be launched the following evening, Tuesday, November 25, but although its leader's health was improving he was still not well enough to take part and so it had to be postponed. The National-Country Party campaign due to open in Brisbane the next night thus became the opening night for the coalition.

'Perhaps you could go up for it, love?' said Malcolm, now burning more from frustration than from fever. 'It'd be such a help.'

So Tam set off by herself to Queensland for the big National-Country Party rally which was to launch the '75 election campaign. She felt rather apprehensive and alone. In the plane on the way up Sir John Atwill, who was then the federal President of the Liberal Party, said: 'Tamie dear, you know you will be asked to say a few words?'

'No! I don't believe it!' she said. 'Oh yes,' said Sir John. 'Just for a few minutes. It's expected of you.'

Tamie took a deep breath. She recalled all the times in her childhood when she had been taught that you can do anything if It's Expected Of You, and gave her mother a mental wink. The only paper in her handbag to write on was a round cardboard *Gough's got to go!* campaign badge. She scribbled a few notes for her speech on the back of it just as the plane touched down at Brisbane airport.

'We had very little time to change,' Tam told me next day. 'Then there I was at Festival Hall. It was packed and there was speaker after speaker and then Doug Anthony came on. Doug's a great rabble rouser. When he gets in front of the microphone he turns on like a switch, throwing his arms around and his words lighting up the audience like a fire. Everything he said bought a tremendous cheer! It gave me the goosebumps. And all the time I'm thinking "*my god*! I can't follow on after this"!' But she did, and the hall erupted. Shouts and cheers and whistles and cries of 'Good on you, Tamie darlin'!' came from everywhere.

Eventually she was allowed to speak. 'Thank you! Thank you!' she said, 'for that overwhelming welcome! I will take back every wave and cheer to Malcolm. He was so disappointed not to be here. He sent his apologies with his nurse—that's me!' More whistles and cheers. 'We have known Doug and Margot Anthony for a long time and over a long period of co-operation. Flying up along the coast of beautiful Australia today, I thought what a lovely place it would be when Malcolm and Doug are both in government together. Malcolm's fever is much better, and he's heading off tomorrow on his campaign trail . . . I am sure Australia too is affected with the fever. Not the fever of Malcolm, but the fever of "Vote Liberal-Country Party!" And with the fever of "Vote Liberal-Country Party!" sweeping the country, I know we will have a wonderful *win* on December 13!' and the hall exploded in thunderous applause.

'Crikey, Tam,' said brother Hugh some time later, when she was regaling the story to the family. ' "The coast of beautiful Australia" and "the fever of vote Liberal-Country Party"—it's not exactly the Gettysburg address, is it?' '*I know*! Don't rub it in!' she groaned. 'And at the end of the evening I went up to one of the party heavies and said sorry my speech was so innane and pathetic. I expected "But Mrs. Fraser, it was wonderful!" but he said, "Don't worry, Tamie dear, it doesn't matter. No-one noticed!" '

One of Tamie's favourite sayings is 'remember, when you're feeling on top of the world, that the earth turns over once every 24 hours.' The morning after the Brisbane rally there came in the mail another death threat for the children. It is superfluous to describe how that affects a mother—or a father. Security was made tighter than ever and the children were in good hands but Tamie and Malcolm were still distressed at the prospect of leaving them to go off on the campaign trail.

'Grandfather,' said Malcolm, on the telephone to Nareeb Nareeb. 'Er, we're having a spot of, you know, trouble down here. It's the kids. Do you think . . . er . . . er . . . would it be possible . . . ?' (The family always smiled at how Malcolm, so fluent on the rostrum, could be so inarticulate over personal matters.) Mum and Dad set off for Melbourne from their home in the western district within the hour. 'Yippee! Grandfather's in charge!' cried Phoebe, aged 9, dashing up the front hall to hug both of them when they arrived.

That night Malcolm and Tamie were cheered wildly as they arrived at Melbourne's Dallas Brooks Hall to launch the Liberal Party election campaign. A huge crowd heard Malcolm pledge sound economic management, an investment-led recovery and reform to the tax system for companies and individuals. 'Unless confidence in private enterprise survives, Australia quite literally faces economic disaster,' he said. A return to the private enterprise principle of reward for individual initiative and hard work was the keystone of his platform, and the next day he and Tam set off around Australia to sell it.

The 1975 election campaign was different from most in recent memory. Although it was the first Tam had experienced as the wife of a party leader she had been involved in election campaigns for years. 'You get a feel for these things,' she said, 'and this one was different.

'The crowds were different. At all the rallies we went to—Sydney, Brisbane, Perth, Adelaide—there was a totally different amalgamation of people. There were old women in pink flowered hats, and young workmen in tin hard-hats, there were accountants and brickies and plumbers, bushies and surfies and clerks.

I mean, sure lots of them were shouting "Gough! Gough! Gough!" but people from every spectrum of Australian society were out there supporting us in that election. In 1983 they were not there.'

During the early days of the campaign, my mother had a problem with her teeth. At that time she wore a plate, details of which I have not the slightest intention of divulging. Suffice to say it was vital to her well-being, and not long after she arrived down at Fairlie Court she was unfortunate enough to break it on a chop bone, and in horror telephoned home to have her spare posted down immediately, if not sooner.

When the parcel arrived, special delivery, priority paid, Mum happened to be out shopping, and she arrived back just in time to find the security officer handing it over, with extreme care, to the police.

'Don't worry, that parcel's quite safe, Officer,' said Mum, as she approached. 'It belongs to me. Could I have it please?'

'Sorry, Mrs. Beggs,' said the security officer. 'But after that letter bomb in Sydney the other day, we can't take any risks.'

'Young man,' said Mum, drawing herself up to her full and considerable height, 'I know you have a job to do, and we all appreciate your efforts. But,' and here she leaned forward and made a quick, clean grab of the parcel from the hands of the astonished security man, 'this parcel contains a highly personal item and I will *not* have a group of soldiers down at the bomb squad howling their eyes out with mirth at my expense when they come to open it. Is that clear?'

'But Mrs. Beggs . . . ' said the officer helplessly.

'Listen, I know you're concerned, and only trying to protect the family', she went on, more gently, 'so I'll tell you what I'll do. I'll take this parcel right down to the bottom of the garden and open it there, quite alone. If you hear a loud explosion you may come and scrape me off the fence and hose me off the geraniums. No-one else's life will be endangered. But I tell you, *no-one* but me is going to open this parcel!' And no-one did.

The pace of the campaign was exhausting. Rallies, tours, street walks, party functions, press briefings, interviews, and an endless succession of official lunches, dinners and even breakfasts. Sleep was a precious luxury and to keep proffering a charming smile as expected was sometimes a major effort. Occasionally it was an impossibility.

'One day during the campaign we were in a pub in Bondi,' said Tamie. 'There was a huge crowd and the police told us to work our way back to the car as things were starting to get nasty. People were milling all around us, yelling "Gough's Gonna Win! Gough's Gonna Win!" in an awful, threatening sort of way. Anyway, I got separated from Malcolm and was trying to fight my way back through the crowd when someone dropped their "Gough's Gonna Win!" banner, and hit me on the head. It was an accident but it hurt like hell and made me absolutely furious!

'I pushed on through the crowd and a chap with a can of beer in both hands and wearing only shorts and thongs came up to me, looked at me kind of sideways, then started shouting: "Gough's gonna win! Gough's gonna win!" Something inside me snapped. I stopped, turned around, looked at him eyeball-to-eyeball, then cried: "Phooey! He's not! He's *bloody well not*!" and I stamped my foot at him. The chap looked at me in astonishment. "Huh, you're game, love," he said, smiling suddenly from ear to ear. Then he bent over and gave me a smacking kiss and disappeared!'

Meanwhile back at Fairlie Court Grandfather was still In Charge but it was an unusual household he presided over. Each morning the children went off to school as usual—with an armed bodyguard trailing close behind. Tamie and Malcolm dashed in and out as their schedule allowed, and all the while Grannie kept the household running, the meals cooked, the clothes clean and the children secure. Mrs Fraser, Malcolm's mother, came over from nearby Domain Road to help whenever she could. But the atmosphere was still tense.

One morning a friend of Tam's called in at Fairlie Court very early to deliver a cake she had made for the family. Not wanting to disturb the household she crept up the path, left the cake on the front doorstep, and slipped away.

Luckily Tam was already up, and on hearing muffled noises glanced out the window to see her friend walking briskly away down the street—and two husky security guards setting out after her at a run. Only Tam's hasty vocal intervention prevented her being arrested.

One day as the campaign progressed Eda telephoned Mum at Fairlie Court to find out how things there were going.

'Quite well, thank you dear,' said Mum in the rather clipped, high-pitched voice she used when things were going quite the opposite.

'So what's happening? What have you been doing?', Eda asked.

'As a matter of fact, I've just been out in the laundry washing the spit from your sister's best silk blouse,' she replied.

The day before Tamie and Malcolm had attended a rally at the Northcote Town Hall, deep in Labor territory. There was a huge crowd and the mood turned ugly. Rotten eggs, tomatoes, empty cans and flour bombs were hurled at them by an angry, screaming mob. They were jostled, heckled and abused. And they were spat on.

One of the Liberal Party organisers of the rally was a new Australian, a migrant from central Europe, and he was terrified. 'I've seen it all before!' he gasped, his face ashen. 'Rule by mob violence! You've got to stop it or it'll all happen again here in this country! You've got to win!'

'It's a funny feeling,' said Tam, years later when she felt able to talk about these things, 'standing up there in front of a sea of faces and thinking maybe someone out there wants to take your life. I used to scan the crowd constantly, watching for any person who looked, well . . . a problem. Mind you,' she said, quickly discharging her fear into humour, as always, 'I'd never worked out what on earth I would do if ever I saw someone actually point a gun at Malcolm. You can't just push him over! I mean, Malcolm wouldn't just fall conveniently to the ground if you gave him bit of a shove. It'd take four beefy policemen in a flying rugby tackle!'

But mostly in that election it was roses, roses all the way, and the Frasers were greeted by cheering, enthusiastic crowds. Meanwhile the press was reporting growing support in the opinion polls. 'Your poll keeps going up, eh Mal?' said brother Hugh, ever master of the single entendre. 'No wonder Tamie's been smiling so much lately!' *'Turn on the lights!'* said the Liberal Party campaign slogan, and all over Australia millions of people obeyed. On city streets and freeways and country roads and tracks supporters everywhere were driving around with their headlights turned full on. The result was, dare I say it, electrifying. Encouraged, Malcolm kept hammering away at the economic issues, inflation, unemployment, and the need to cut government spending and re-direct resources back to the private sector.

About three days before the election, a letter came in the mail for Tamie which took her breath away. It was from Sir Robert Menzies.

My very dear Tamie,

May an old campaigner tell you how much he admires what you have been doing in the course of this campaign. You have not only handled your interviews with great charm and skill, but you have been of tremendous assistance to Malcolm.

I am now convinced that he will win on Saturday. I would like you to convey to him my belief that this will be a great personal triumph, a complete vindication of his character and attainments.

I notice that some people have been promoting themselves for future consideration in a rather curious way. Do get Malcolm to believe, as is the truth, that his personal prestige will be so great that he can exercise his choice of Ministers without feeling that he must please anybody but himself. It is essential that the new government should be competent and cohesive, for the work they will have to do will be of extreme difficulty. Don't let Malcolm be too modest about it all. In my opinion, he will have the same amount of personal authority and prestige as I always hoped for in my own case in my own time.

Thank you both for the invitation for Saturday night. I will be at home. I cannot face the idea of being questioned by a mob of one-sided newspapermen at the gathering you have arranged at the Southern Cross Hotel. But you will know where my thoughts are because this is, in my opinion, the most vital Australian election in my time.

With warmest regards to you both,
Yours sincerely,
Robert Menzies.

The last meeting of the election campaign was held in Warrnambool in western Victoria on Friday, December 12, true to the Frasers' lifelong practice of beginning and ending all their campaigns in their home electorate of Wannon. Next day, polling day, they spent Going Around the Traps. This meant visiting as many polling booths in their electorate as possible, to meet the officials, thank all the Liberal Party workers for their help, and to shake hands with any casual voters who appeared on the scene. Portland, Warrambool, Heywood, Casterton, Coleraine and then—Nareen. 'We ourselves always voted at Nareen,' said Tamie. 'The polling booth is in a tiny little old stone hall, and quite a crowd of local people had gathered there to wish us well. I was thrilled to vote for Malcolm, but I was always embarrassed at him voting for himself!'

After lunch at their Nareen homestead with the press who had been travelling with them, they drove to Hamilton, visited the polling booths there, then flew on to Melbourne to where their children, some family and a few close friends—and their future—awaited them.

Their future did not take long to unfold. After what my mother called A Quick Scratch Meal (three beautiful courses—but eaten standing up), everyone turned their attention to the television where the first results were starting to trickle in from polling booths all over the country. Almost immediately there showed a movement of support towards the Coalition. About nine o'clock Mark, who had been standing by his father most of the evening, lent over and said quietly: 'Reckon it's safe to give you this now, Dad, you've got it in the bag,' and he pressed a crumpled brown paper parcel into his father's hands. 'Good shot for the election!' The parcel contained a champagne glass and Malcolm was immensely touched by the gesture. He didn't say much but there was no need for words between them.

Meanwhile the television was reporting to the nation that the movement of support had turned into a landslide. About 10.30 the household made its way to the Southern Cross hotel where Tamie and Malcolm were greeted with thunderous cheers and applause from the waiting crowds of supporters and staff. Back home in the country we were in a fever of joy and excitement, living through every moment with them. By midnight I could restrain myself no longer and reached for the 'phone.

'It's fantastic, Mal!' I said. 'How are you both? How's the Body Politic?'

'To tell the truth, about buggered!' he replied laughing, and through his elation I could hear the depths of his tiredness. As my mother remarked later when they eventually all arrived back at Fairlie Court, by anyone's standards it had been A Very Big Day. The future now lay open before them, full of opportunity and bright promise, fears and awesome responsibilities. But for the moment all they could think of was days and days of deep and dreamless sleep.

Wishful thinking. First thing next morning the new PM was launched into a frenetic round of press conferences, meetings, briefings, consultations and discussions. This was just Day One—but the show was on the road.

Chapter 3
THE LODGE

The Fraser family moved into The Lodge towards the end of January, 1976—all except for Mark, who had started work as a jackaroo on a sheep station in the Riverina region of New South Wales. Mark was still 17, Angela 16, Hugh 13, and Phoebe only nine.

'Yes, she was little, really little to have to handle the whole thing of being the daughter of a Prime Minister,' said Tam. 'For instance, she had never had the experience of being waited on at table—actually, none of the children had. Anyway, the first night at dinner we all sat down in the dining room and the maid brought us our meal and Phoebe was so overcome at the whole procedure that she suddenly started calling Malcolm "Papa". All her life until that time she'd only ever called him "Dad" or "Daddy", but she must have felt the occasion warranted something special and perhaps had read the term in a book or heard it on TV or something. Anyway, it instantly dissolved the rest of the family into laughter, including Phoebe and her "Papa", and relaxed the situation completely.'

When Tamie entered the Lodge that first day she found a letter addressed to her sitting on the table in the front hall. It was a note from Margaret Whitlam welcoming her to The Lodge, wishing her well and hoping she and her family would be as happy there as the Whitlams had been.

Thinking back over all the bitterness that had gone

before, Tamie was touched by the gesture, and was to repeat it herself when she moved out of The Lodge to make way for Hazel Hawke in 1983.

But apart from that there was no sign that the house ever had been inhabited by a Prime Minister. There were no records, no historical artifacts or memorabilia, none of the trappings of office. 'I thought there'd be furniture steeped in history, paintings which could tell a thousand stories of leaders past, but there was nothing,' said Tamie. 'It wasn't even particularly Australian in atmosphere.' It became one of Tam long term aims, as Prime Minister's wife, to change all that.

However, the staff she inherited were wonderful. 'From the very beginning we had no secrets, because one of the staff there, Mrs. Tomic, used to help me years before when the children were small and we lived in Canberra, and Angela had once sicked her wedding ring up on the stairs!' said Tamie. 'Mrs. Tomic had taken it off to clean the bath or something and Angela, who was only about two at the time, was playing around with it and swallowed it. We had no idea! Mrs. Tomic hadn't even missed it until we found it there gleaming amongst Angela's mess in the middle of the stairs! Anyway, it felt wonderful to get to The Lodge and find Mrs. Tomic there to look after us again.'

How can I describe The Lodge? Christopher and I visited there only twice, and briefly, during the seven and a half years the Frasers were there, and on each occasion we had such a wonderful time that I find it hard to be objective. But, to be honest, considering it is Australia's White House, the nation's No. 10, we were not over-impressed. Apart from being inefficient in a functional sense, parts of the house were almost shabby. The principal guest room (well, there were only two), where we slept had wall-paper peeling off the ceiling and there were numerous cracks up the bathroom walls. One evening when Chris was having a shower, the shower rose fell off and a jet of water spurted everywhere. 'You're wrong about this place, you know, Tam,' he said when he came down to dinner. 'There is something historical here. It's the plumbing!'

The night we arrived Malcolm had been away all day in Parliament and was not expected back until later on that night. Tam and we two had a merry old dinner together, with Chris and I solemnly addressing her throughout as 'Tamara' (we had heard about Phoebe's 'Papa') much to her chagrin, and we had just gone up to bed about ten-thirty when Malcolm arrived back and came on up to say hello.

We hadn't been married long and he took one look at the arrangements in our room—two single beds set wide apart with a heavy oak table with some books and flowers on in between—and said: 'This won't do for a holiday! C'mon, Tam. Give me a hand!' Grunting and groaning he dragged the table over to the other side of the room, narrowly avoiding spilling the flowers all over the carpet, then heaved the two single beds until they were pushed together, making one big, wide, and wonderfully luxurious double-bed. And neither our mirth nor our heartfelt appeals to leave things alone could persuade him to change it all back.

Next morning when the maid came in with our breakfast, she nearly dropped the tray. It took the most enormous amount of self control, but I am proud to say I had the strength of character not to explain our change of decor, and suffered in dignified silence when she continued to look at us knowingly for the rest of our visit.

While we were there Mark drove down from Denniliquin for a night to see his parents at The Lodge. We all had dinner together with Bryan George, the new butler, looking after us and after dinner Bryan asked Mark what would he like to drink with his coffee. 'I'll 'ave a beer, thanks,' said Mark, very much the big jackaroo.

'Darling, why not try a little glass of port or a liqueur?' said Tam. 'Those are the kinds of drinks you have after dinner.'

'No thanks, I'll just 'ave a beer,' said Mark.

'Certainly,' said Bryan. He returned a few moments

later and to our great enjoyment handed Mark on a silver tray his beer—served in a liqueur glass.

The Lodge was designed by architects Oakley & Parkes of Melbourne at the behest of the Federal Capital Commission as 'a temporary official residence for the Prime Minister'. It was originally intended that The Lodge 'would be occupied by the Prime Minister until such time as a permanent monumental Prime Minister's residence is constructed, and thereafter to be used for other official purposes such as for the President of the Senate or Speaker of the House of Representatives'. In 1926, under the supervision of Oakley & Parkes, James Taylor of Glebe, NSW, built The Lodge for a cost of £28,319—which included developing the grounds from bare paddock to an effective garden of lawns, plantations, shrubberies, a tennis court and a croquet lawn, plus furniture and furnishings chosen by interior decorator, Mrs. Ruth Lane Poole.

Stanley Bruce was the first Prime Minister to occupy The Lodge but James Scullin would not live there in 1929 as he thought it was too grand! So consideration was given to letting the building, but no tender was received. It was also suggested at this time that the building could become the home of the National Library or perhaps a private hospital, but nothing ever came of these suggestions, and with the election of the Lyons Government in 1931 The Lodge was reoccupied.

One of the problems with The Lodge was its size. The reception rooms downstairs consisted of the front hall, the dining-room, the drawing room which was two rooms opening into each other and a small office for the PM. 'If the children were there with some friends and Malcolm came home with some people he wanted to talk to he'd have to kick the children out of the sitting-room—and there was nowhere else for them to go.'

The dining-room sat ten comfortably, 12 at a squash, and this made official entertaining difficult. 'For instance at most political dinners you'd have to have the visiting PM and his wife, our PM and his wife; their

Foreign Minister and his wife, and our Foreign Minister and his wife; their Ambassador to our country and his wife, and our Ambassador to their country and his wife—that's 12,' said Tamie, 'and most of those people had been together all day anyway!

'So what I used to do in the early days before we had the dining-room enlarged was have the Hard Core to dinner, and invite some other people in for a sort of supper afterwards, arriving at nine o'clock and staying until about ten-thirty. That way it gave an opportunity for some other people to meet the heavies— and of course the heavies to meet a few people other than the party they were working with.'

Apart from being small for its purpose The Lodge was also ill-equipped. There had been no new plates bought for The Lodge since the very first dinner service purchased by Mr. Stanley Bruce in 1927. When the Frasers moved in there were no longer enough flat, middle-sized plates to allow for 12 people to have an entree and then pudding without the plates being washed in between. 'If it was a very busy night for the staff we'd have soup,' said Tamie, 'but really it seemed ridiculous if you always had to have soup at official dinners. So I ordered some more plates, and there was a terrible stink about the extravagance. It made me furious.'

The plates were ordered from Royal Doulton's Melbourne office, and interestingly the man who took the order when it was finally placed in 1976 was the same man, a junior office boy in those days, who had taken the original order in 1926. 'Exactly 50 years had elapsed, and this was his last order before he retired,' said Tamie. 'The pattern had been designed originally specially for the Prime Minister of Australia, and I re-ordered it from Royal Doulton because I only wanted plates that would match, rather than a whole new set.'

The service areas of The Lodge were inadequate also. The laundry was downstairs outside and the drier was upstairs inside. 'You had to cart the sheets from the laundry outside the back door all the way up the outside stairs in the wind and rain, through the staff sitting-room and through to another dingy little pozzie where someone had stuck the drier. I mean, the whole thing was impossibly antiquated and inefficient, it just wasn't fair on the staff, and that was why I battled and battled and finally got clearance to have it done up.'

This time Tam knew there would be a fuss, and she handled matters differently. The trouble was no Prime Minister liked spending money on The Lodge as he was perceived to be spending it on himself. One of Tam's long-term aims was to try and change the general public's attitude to all the official establishments so that Australians would regard them as belonging to the nation as a whole rather than thinking they were just a personal perk of the current Prime Minister, and thus would take a pride in them being Right.

Another problem was that there had never been anyone with overall official responsibility for these buildings. Thus at The Lodge there was no inventory, no guidelines, no continuity of maintenance or management. 'I mean, when the tiles were leaking you got someone to fix them,' said Tamie, 'but there was no-one to see that it was done before they leaked. When we arrived the paint was peeling off all the window frames. I had to go to Malcolm and he had to go to his department and organise someone to see to it. Now the Prime Minister shouldn't have to worry about peeling window frames. It should just function. That's why we started the Official Establishments Trust.'

The Committee on Official Establishments, as it became known, was an apolitical committee set up in September, 1976, to be responsible for the care, maintenance and development of the four official establishments—The Lodge; Government House, Canberra; Kirribilli and Admiralty House in Sydney. Its initial job was to investigate the present condition of the four official establishments, and also to inquire into 'the type of establishment and facilities required to enable the proper operations of the Governor General, the Prime Minister, and VIPs using the establishments as official guests of the Commonwealth Government.'

The report and recommendations of this Committee were released in December, 1977. '*Lodge Conditions Appalling!*' was the headline next day in *The Canberra Times*. 'According to a report tabled in Parliament yesterday, staff employed at the Prime Minister's official Canberra residence, The Lodge, live in appalling and out-of-date conditions,' the paper said. Enough said. Tamie's renovations were carried out.

Chapter 4
THE HOSTESS

At first, Tamie found life in The Lodge rather lonely. The three younger children had gone off to boarding school and she missed their company and constant demands. 'That was one of the hardest times for me, personally. There I was with a marvellous secretary and staff, people everywhere in fact, and lonely as hell. After all those years of having four children to look after, and so often on my own, then suddenly none—it was so empty!'

The Frasers had been advised that if their children went to school each day in Canberra from The Lodge they would have to be accompanied by a bodyguard. 'And that's no way for a child to live,' said Tam. 'We were scared stiff that they'd grow either to resent their security guard bitterly, or else, worse still, become dependant on him. Either way it was not a normal way to grow up, so we thought boarding school was the best answer. But Phoebe was only nine, and it was a very difficult decision.'

The newly-elected Parliament was now sitting and Malcolm was spending most of his time at the House, working incredible hours and deeply pre-occupied with what he was learning about the state of the economy. 'I remember him coming home one night very late, everything drooping. He said: "I knew before we got in that the economy was in bad shape, but I had no idea how bad. God knows if we can ever pull it out." '

But life gathered momentum with remarkable speed and soon Tam had no time for wallowing. In the first week of parliament, as had been the practice in past years, she held a luncheon at The Lodge for the wives of all MPs. 'It was not a fun affair,' said Tam. 'There was a lot of residual bitterness over Mr. Whitlam's sacking and, despite the fact we'd just won an election by the greatest margin in history, many people in the Labor Party still would not accept us and many Labor wives decided to boycott my lunch. But Mrs. Whitlam came and Mrs. Crean, and there were some others too, and I thought it was brave and decent of them.'

Not long afterwards, Tam played hostess to her first official overseas visitors. 'I'll never forget the day King Hussein arrived', she told me over lunch one day in Melbourne. 'We had to go out and greet him and Queen Alia at the airport. Now meeting people with Malcolm was always a nightmare. I went over to Parliament House well beforehand, knowing it would take us 14 minutes to get to the airport, and Malcolm thought two minutes before we were due to leave that he had time to make another 'phone call—which took five or six minutes! Then we rushed downstairs and the motorcycle escort were vvrrrooming their engines ready to roar off and we leapt into our car and Noel, our driver, roared off behind them.

'Malcolm was saying "Hurry up! Hurry up! We're running late! We've got to get there on time" and we were just rolling along nicely when he said: "You can't push people off the road! You can't push people off the road! Slow down, Noel! Slow down!" And so we slowed down. He had this thing about it, you see, officials in big shiny cars pushing people off the road. He hated it. He thought it was un-Australian.

'Anyway, the motorcycles were now half a mile ahead and they slowed down so we could catch up to them, then Malcolm started again, saying: "We're going to be late! Speed up! Noel, speed up! No, no! We can't push people off the road!" and this went on all the way to the airport. I rocked back and forth with my neck nearly breaking off at the seam!

'We finally arrived out there just as the plane was landing,' said Tam, 'so we all stood out on the tarmac and as the plane rolled up the national anthems were played and Malcolm took the salute. Then they let off the 21 guns. Now I simply can't stand still when they let off those guns. I jump out of my skin—every time! But Jim Scholtens, the chief of protocol in the PM's department, used to be angelic and sort of wedge himself against me when it began, to stop me leaping in the air every time a gun went *boom*! and falling off my high heels.

'The King and Queen of Jordan were given the full ceremonial welcome, and returning from the airport we travelled in convoy. There was an Australian security car out in front, then the King's motorcycle outriders, then the King's car, then the King's security car, then our motorcycle outriders, then us, etc. etc— you can imagine the sort of cavalcade it was—and we all drove along at about 30 miles an hour. Now up ahead a civilian car coming towards us pulled over to the side of the road and parked in the ditch in order to watch the cavalcade as it went by. Malcolm, misreading their actions completely, said: "We can't push people off the road! Stop, Noel! Stop the car!" So we stopped and Malcolm leapt out and strode over to the astonished people and said: "I'm terribly sorry we pushed you off the road. I do apologise," then walked back and got in the car again and off we went.'

'Meanwhile, King Hussein's contingent thought there'd been an assassination attempt! The King and Queen ducked below window level and were driven away at high speed. A security van stopped and spilled out all its guards who took up their positions, legs apart, guns at the ready, up and down the road. We drove nonchanlantly up and explained that no, there was no emergency, everything was fine, we'd just been held up briefly, apologising to some people for pushing them off the road. The Jordanians shook their heads in disbelief! Australians were a very strange race!'

A few days later Tamie held a women's luncheon

at The Lodge for Queen Alia, 'and it was a complete disaster,' she told me. It was to be held on Ash Wednesday so she had decided that fish would be the safest thing to serve. Her secretary, Susannah Law-Smith, checked the matter with Queen Alia's protocol officer as is customary, and was told no problem. But as it happened, the chef at The Lodge had left two days before and was not yet replaced, so Tam ordered the fish, beautiful Port Philip whiting, from outside caterers.

It looked quite scrumptious when it arrived but when it was served to Queen Alia, she glanced at it and said: 'I'm terribly sorry, but I'm allergic to fish.'

'My whole world fell apart around my ears!' Tam told us. 'There she sat in her Valentino coat looking stunning, saying, "I'm terribly sorry, but I'm allergic to fish." *There was nothing else in the house but fish*!', and Tamie rolled her eyes in horror at the recollection. 'Then I thought, there must be a few eggs in the 'fridge left over from breakfast. Would you prefer an omelette, Your Highness? I said, and she said "thank you, that would be lovely." But of course there was no-one out in the kitchen to cook it. I could hardly say, excuse me, while I just pop out for a second and whip it up for you.'

In desperation Tamie turned and called to Bryan the butler, who at the time was busy serving drinks. 'Bryan,' she said, fixing him with a level, piercing gaze, 'would you please go out to the kitchen and ask chef to make an omelette for Her Highness?'

'Certainly, Mrs Fraser. At once!' said Bryan, without so much as a blink of the eye. Five minutes later he returned from the kitchen and placed a steaming and elegantly garnished omelette before Queen Alia, and Tamie made a mental note to tell Malcolm an OBE or even a knighthood would not be inappropriate.

Tam began to recall other disastrous dinners in a distinguished list of crises.

'Do you remember the time way back when Malcolm was Minister for Defence and we lived in Daly Street (Canberra)—I had a Moslem woman to lunch?

I'd decided that for starters we'd have tomato soup, Paradise Soup it's called, with cucumber and melon balls for garnish—but then we couldn't get any melons so we used strips of ham instead. It was one of my favourites at the time. Then we thought we'd have chicken, that would be safe, and some safe pud too. But when the soup was served my guest of honour took one look at it and said: "But zis is zee *pig*! I do not eat *zee pig*!" and shoved her plate away with such passion she sent the salts and peppers flying all over the table. So I said I'm terribly sorry, I do apologise, and beckoned the maid over and murmured: "Please could you take this away and bring Madame just some plain tomato?" Of course I meant some plain tomato *soup*, i.e. without the ham. But when the maid returned she placed in front of my distinguished guest a plain tomato full stop—sliced in a soup bowl, and quite without any herb, garnish or condiment!'

'So what did you do?'

'Nothing!' she said. 'One thing I have learned over the years is: try to explain and you only get in deeper! But I did relate the story to Bryan, the butler when we were having some more people who were Muslims to lunch at The Lodge. I'd chosen the menu very carefully this time, and on the day I was sitting up there at the dining-table talking away super-animatedly to my guest and I didn't take any notice when Bryan put my food down in front of me until I heard him murmur, very softly so no-one else could hear: "Some ham, Mrs. Fraser?"

'I froze! My blood turned to ice! I tore my eyes away from the face of my guest of honour, where they'd been transfixed in horror, and glanced down at my plate—to find five pieces of juicy, steaming asparagus—as ordered. I took a long time to forgive Bryan for that. It was a terrible moment!'

Bryan and the kitchen staff, with whom Tamie had built up a great sense of cameraderie in trying to do the Right Thing for Australia when entertaining overseas guests, enjoyed her visible flinch to the full.

Chapter 5
TO THE EAST

In June, 1976, the Frasers made an official visit to Japan and China. The trip covered 25,000 miles and lasted for two weeks.

'We landed in Tokyo on Tuesday, June 15, but officially arrived the next day on Wednesday, June 16!' said Tam. 'It was such a good idea. Instead of greeting Mr. and Mrs. Miki with swollen ankles, crushed clothes and electric hair, we all had time to recover from the long flight and arrive pristine and presentable!' There were about twenty people travelling with the Frasers in the official Australian touring party. 'Andrew Peacock was with us,' said Tam, 'and John Menadue, the head of the PM's department, and Alan Renouf, head of Foreign Affairs, plus advisers, secretaries and press officers, security staff and our doctor, Dr. Ray.' Also travelling with them to cover the trip were numerous members of the Australian press corps.

Protocol is always important, but especially so in Asia, and Tamie did her homework carefully. The form was to be that after they had been officially welcomed by the Japanese Prime Minister at the Akasaka Palace, Malcolm would step forward and introduce Mr. Miki to the Australian contingent, and Tamie was to introduce Mrs. Miki. She already knew most of the Australian party and with those she didn't know she carefully memorised both their names and where they would be standing in line during the ceremony.

'Everything went swimmingly. There were flags flying, a guard of honour and massed bands playing "Waltzing Matilda" which made us all very misty-eyed. It is the most Australian thing you can hear when you're abroad. Then when the time came, I reeled off everyone's name with the greatest aplomb until I reached the very end of the line—and there was a man, an Australian, whom I'd never seen in my life before! He was an utter stranger! Certainly not on my list.

'Anyway, I took a deep breath, looked him squarely in the eye, and said: 'Mrs. Miki, may I introduce Mr., er, Robinson?'. He looked a bit stunned, but only for an instant. Then he said very gravely: 'How do you do, Mrs. Miki.' Later on that night Tamie saw 'Mr Robinson' at a reception and rushed up to him, and said: 'Who the hell are you anyway?' They both laughed about the incident and Tamie expressed her heartfelt thanks to him for not letting her down.

In Tokyo the Frasers stayed at the Akasaka Palace, a sumptuous miniature Versailles recently re-decorated in the style of Louis Quinze. It was full of massive chandeliers, gilt-edged mirrors, carved marble fireplaces, and gold-painted furniture a la Louis Quinze all covered in rich, pink silk brocades. On the walls the dadoes, cornices and architraves glowed with gold leaf. The floors were a lush expanse of soft pink carpet.

With typical Japanese thoroughness, their hosts had taken note of how tall the Frasers are, and provided them with a double-bed fully eight feet long and eight feet wide with an enormous pink silk brocade studded bedhead. It was the talk of the Australian camp once the word got around.

The first morning in Tokyo Tamie and Malcolm were awoken at 6am by the sound of rattling glass. Tamie opened her eyes and looked up in disbelief! The huge chandelier hanging from the middle of the ceiling above their bed was swaying from side to side, its myriad glass pieces jangling loudly in protest. An earthquake was shaking the building. It was not a major one, but it was disconcerting at the time. So were the rumours later on regarding it and the Frasers' giant double bed.

In the gardens of the Akasaka Palace there was a Japanese pavilion where Tamie and Malcolm were taken one afternoon for tea. 'It was very spare with beautiful lines,' said Tamie. 'Along a wall there would be one single painting or one single but exquisite arrangement of flowers. It had the same feeling of space and serenity that the Japanese seem to achieve in their gardens. I suppose in a country which is small and crowded their culture has evolved that way through necessity.'

Japan is now a highly cosmopolitan society and this was reflected in their official entertaining. 'They were wonderful hosts,' said Tam. 'One day we were taken to a Japanese-style inn called "Ryuguden" near Lake Ashi, overlooking Mount Fuji, and given a truly authentic Japanese meal. I remember the pudding best. It was in the shape of a hydrangea, blue, and so delicate, with all the little florets of a hydrangea perfectly formed in a clear fondant-like substance. It tasted very sweet, but looked quite the most beautiful thing you've ever seen on a plate.' There were little cushions on the floor to sit on and the table had been raised just a fraction so the large Australian visitors could get their legs underneath.

'As I sat down and made myself comfortable I saw suddenly appearing on the other side of the table two awfully nasty toes—my own! They looked so enormous and so dreadful that I withdrew them hastily and for the sake of Australia sat on them in agony for the rest of the luncheon.

'Whenever we visited a temple or a shrine we had to take off our shoes and leave them at the door. The Japanese with typical politeness would ask what size we wore so they could provide little slippers for us. I was always too embarrassed to give my true size and said two sizes smaller, so my little slippers never fitted me! And you should have seen the shoes left behind at the temple door. A row of dainty little ones like dolls shoes and then two huge pairs—Malcolm's and mine. It looked like Mr. and Mrs. Gulliver's Travels!'

Security was strictly enforced at all times. One morning when Malcolm was away on official talks and Tamie had some spare time, she asked if she might have a wander around the gardens at the Akasaka Palace. Certainly, said her hosts, so off she went anxious to absorb the tranquility of the gardens and commune with nature—only to find she had 14 security guards tagging along behind to share the experience.

Another afternoon when Malcolm was again busy with meetings Tam was taken to see a big Tokyo department store. 'The Japanese are so polite and lots of people always went along with you,' said Tam. 'On this particular outing Susannah Law-Smith, my secretary, and I were the only visitors going, but we had a positive entourage of officials' wives and diplomats' wives, and protocol officers and of course the usual army of security guards along with us.'

When they reached the store they were amazed to find it empty of all but a few customers. 'It was done for security reasons of course,' said Tam, 'but with three or four eager and smiling sales girls behind each counter bowing every time I passed by, there was no way I could merely browse through the merchandise.' Tamie had no money with her, but Susannah was able to come to the rescue. 'So then I swept through the store saying I'll have one of these and I'll have one of those and when I came to the kimonos I said I'll have 10 of those, and all the time Susannah was following me around paying for everything, and murmuring Yes Queen and No Queen until eventually she ran out of money and we had to stop, but not before I must have single-handedly reversed the balance of trade!'

The Frasers and their travelling party flew on to Peking, China, on Sunday June 20, where they were greeted by a tumultuous welcome at the airport. Flags fluttered all around and massed columns of soldiers paraded up and down. Thousands of brightly-clad school children cried 'Welcome, warmly welcome!'

in Chinese at the top of their lungs as they danced around in formations of breath-taking precision on the tarmac in front of the official party. 'It was a positive barrage of colour and sound and movement,' said Tamie. 'You felt quite battered with welcome just standing there watching.'

The scene was in marked contrast to what awaited them in Peking City. There the streets were sombre and subdued and the people were all dressed in dark blue or gray. As the Australian party drove by they waved and smiled, but their smiles seemed automatic, mechanical, Tamie thought, as if merely in response to orders from the state. 'We received these same mechanical smiles wherever we went, and it's not hard to see why. When you're a visitor, driving around a city or being shown through a factory very often you are listening to what you are being told and you are not looking at the people in the streets or behind the machines in a how-do-you-do sort of way. Your glance tends to drift over them. I think the people there felt they were being looked over as just another exhibit, part of the scenery or the equipment so-to-speak.

'It became a real challenge to me to see if I could get from them a proper human response. Wherever I could I made a point of stopping and looking at them directly in the eye, and smiling and saying: 'Hullo! It's so good to be here!' or something—and their faces would light up, so full of warmth and surprise! And interestingly, the further we went from Peking, the easier it became.'

To someone as voluble as Tamie the language barrier in China was rather frustrating. None of the Chinese officials with whom they travelled spoke English and Tamie spoke no Chinese! All communication took place through interpreters. 'And it's so painfully slow!' said Tamie. 'I mean, you get up in the morning and go out to the car and your hostess is there waiting and you say: "Isn't it a beautiful morning?" and the interpretor says: "&%?@+◇<▶>&£>)*&?" and your hostess nods nods and replies: "@▲$%39*<~☎39% $@▲?" to the interpreter who turns to you again and says: "Yes, isn't it a beautiful morning!" and by the time the answer comes back you're painfully aware it wasn't a particularly scintillating particle of conversation anyway. But you can't just stand around with a group of people and all say nothing.'

I asked Malcolm how he had fared negotiating matters of High State through an interpreter. 'Oh, it's easy!' he laughed. 'You get twice the time to think up your reply!' The interpreters, usually women, were strictly professional in approach, keeping their distance, and in no way to be treated as one of the party. Occasionally Tamie would try to talk to them, ask a question of them personally rather than of the official for whom they were interpreting, but they would always pass the question on. 'And if you asked anyone at all a question which was slightly probing, or slightly off the beaten track—perhaps about China's past political structure—the answer would come back: "Isn't it a lovely day?"—something wonderfully polite and totally irrelevant.'

Another thing Tamie noted with interest was that none of the Chinese ever questioned her, either about Australia in general or herself in particular. 'Except once up in the far provinces where the people seemed more open and relaxed—a woman up there asked me did I have any children and I said yes, four. "Oh," she said. "Then you are planning!" and having read about Chinese "planning" I thought she was going to ask me all the gory details of my personal "planning", which through an interpreter was going to be impossibly lengthy, complicated and embarrassing! But luckily she didn't pursue the issue.'

The security the Chinese provided was highly efficient but also extraordinarily discreet, Malcolm told me. 'A Chinese general went through every door before I did, but so unobtrusively that most of the time I was unaware of it. And the courtesy and thoughtfulness of the Chinese as hosts was probably greater than any other country we'd been to.'

Chairman Mao was ill at the time of the Frasers' visit and wherever they travelled throughout China they inquired about his health. 'And we always received exactly the same answer: Chairman Mao is very advanced in years and has enjoyed good health,' said Tamie. Everywhere we went, all over this vast land with billions of people, and always the same set phrase: "Chairman Mao is very advanced in years and has enjoyed good health". It was spooky to think of the organisation and the regimentation which could produce that.'

The first night the Frasers arrived in Peking a gala banquet for 500 people was held in the Great Hall of the People in their honour. 'The entrance to the Great Hall was lined with huge pillars, two by two, and at the base of each pillar stood a piece of oriental art. There were two great blue Ming dogs before the first set of pillars, then two wonderful Cloisonne vases before the next etc. Beside each of these treasures on the floor looking rather incongruous sat a white enamel blue-rimmed spitoon.'

The banquet was a grand occasion. Tamie was seated beside Hua Kuo-feng, the Premier of China, and her interpreter was seated just behind. Malcolm was on the other side. There were 50 round tables all seating 10 people and except for the Australian visitors and some diplomats all the guests were dressed in dark grey or blue Mao jackets.

'One of the courses served at the banquet was a sort of fish soup made from carp,' said Tam. 'It was a mass of tiny sharp bones and I was fascinated to see how the Chinese woman sitting opposite me would manage to eat it. She lifted up her little bowl and scooped a huge blob into her mouth with her chopsticks, then munched it up and swilled it around in her mouth to suck all the juices out, then scooped up another mouthful and another. All the time the lump in her cheek was growing bigger and bigger. I knew she couldn't swallow it and I watched transfixed to see what she would do. Suddenly she rolled the lump out from her cheek into the centre of her mouth and shied it plonk! clean as a whistle into an empty plate in the middle of the table! And she did that four times! I was so impressed never having been able to clear even my gumboot in spitting competitions when we were children!'

There were about nine courses altogether and Tamie's country appetite stood her in good stead. 'But interestingly, Chinese food doesn't make you feel sick if you eat too much of it, whereas with European food if you had nine courses you'd explode well before the seventh. Also, we were advised by Protocol that in China you musn't finish everything on your plate because that means they haven't given you enough. It's good manners to leave some food—unlike in Europe or Australia where it's bad manners because it means you haven't enjoyed it.'

During their visit the Australians were given many different taste sensations. 'We were given sheep's head, webbed feet of ducks, tortoise, jellyfish and starfish. It was all delicious,' said Tam. 'All except the sea slug. I wasn't mad about that. Neither was I too keen on their drink called Moa Tai, a white spirit which the Chinese use to toast each other with all the time. They say "Goombay! Goombay!" and toss it back, and I only tried tossing it back once and it tasted like methylated spirits you've done the washing up in.'

One day the Australians were taken to see the Great Wall of China. 'Quite a long section has been restored and we walked all the way along it,' Tam said. 'Our Chinese hosts said we were very fit to make the distance! I had on good old Sensible Shoes but Malcolm had on his ordinary shoes with leather soles, and the stones were so smooth and worn by generations that he kept taking one step forwards and sliding two steps backwards—which I thought was a very bad thing for a Prime Minister to do. So he took his shoes off and walked on in his socks. When we reached the end of that section we could see the Wall stretching on for miles and miles, snaking through the hills, and it gave such an impression of timelessness and history.'

In Peking Malcolm attended talks with Premier Hua Kuo-feng about trade links and Soviet expansionism in the Indian Ocean. 'It was very important to establish a good relationship as China was becoming an increasingly important market,' Malcolm said. 'And they had a similar view to the Soviet Union as I did, so we got on very well.' While Malcolm was attending official meetings Tamie was taken to visit a kindergarten where children were sent from the age of three to about six. 'It was one of the most interesting things for me,' said Tam. 'The children board there six days a week. Their parents, who are away working, see them only one day a week. I was fascinated to know what effect this had on the strength and unity of the family, but no-one would discuss it with me—except for a woman in Canton (we found Canton much less regimented than Peking) who said early separation from parents had no effect whatsoever. But she answered my question with such vehemence,' said Tam, 'I mean, she almost flew at me, that it made me think that perhaps, well, the subject must have been anxiously discussed many times.'

After three days in Peking, the Australian party boarded a train and travelled to Tai Kiang in Shansi Province, then on to Urumchi, a city at the foothills of the mountain range which runs along the Sino-Russian border. This was a very remote area of Northern China and it was a great honour to be taken there. Everywhere the Australians went people pointed at them and stared. 'In the towns the roads were lined deep with people and as they looked at us you could see their surprise "Oh, there's one! And there's one!" They'd seen so few foreigners through in recent years that we were stared at like people in a zoo. Susannah, my secretary, was a great hit with her long blonde hair. People kept wanting to stroke it to see if it were real!'

In Urumchi the party stayed in an old guest house which had had no other visitors for 10 years—again a special privilege. 'When I turned on the tap in the bathroom to run a bath, stones came out. I don't mean merely gravel, I mean *stones*!' said Tamie. 'So I scooped the stones out of the plughole in handfuls and put them on the floor (there was nowhere else), then I ran the tap again and this time gravel came out but it was still too big to wash down the plughole, so I scooped that out too and put in on the floor. Next time I ran the tap gritty sand came out. By this time I was getting rather short of time for changing for dinner, so the next time, when sort of fine sand came out, I just sat in the bath and pretended I was at the beach!'

Next day the Australians were driven out into the surrounding countryside. It was steep and very harsh. They were taken to see a Yurt, a round felt tent about 20 feet across used by the Mongolian farmers as they move up and down the mountains following the seasons. 'It was the home of the woman who hosted us for the day,' said Tamie. 'She was tiny—she could easily have run backwards and forwards through Malcolm's legs with a big hat on. Her tent was wonderful. Inside was some of the finest hand-woven embroidery I've ever seen. The rug was hand-woven silk; the coverlets on the beds were hand-woven and all exquisitely fine. It was beautiful.'

Tamie and Malcolm sat on cushions on the floor of the Yurt and plates of local delicacies were brought in for them to eat. 'Malcolm took a big blob of a sort of cheese made from fermented mare's milk which I think he mistook for icecream,' said Tamie. 'It was full of ammonia and after about three chews it started to come out his eye balls and his ear holes and his nostrils! But he restrained himself with true Prime Ministerial self-discipline, and eventually managed to gulp it all down.'

Tamie discovered that her experience of boarding school life was a distinct advantage in that situation. She was able to take a good-sized bite of whatever, make the right appreciative faces and schlurp schlurp noises, then in a motion faster than the eye could see palm the remaining portion and transfer it safely to her raincoat pocket.

Another day the Australians were taken right up high into the mountains to visit a lake. The terrain was sheer and scattered with dark grey rocks which glistened like slate in the rain. The vegetation was sparse and the road agonisingly winding and steep. 'It was the most frightening trip I've ever made!' said Tamie. 'We were driven along in huge black cars and the road was all mud and slush from the rain and so narrow that all I could see out the side window was the rocky valley 2000 feet below.

'So I kept my eyes firmly fixed on the road ahead and everytime we came to a hairpin bend it would disappear under the front headlight, then under the front wheel then under the whole of the front of the car and I'd be sitting in the back thinking This is *it*! This is really *it*! then suddenly the road would appear once more from under the front bonnet as we came out of the corner, and we'd thunder on. It was quite terrifying. I just sat there clinging to Malcolm and asking God to look after the children.'

When the party arrived at the top of the mountain pass, they came to a beautiful lake on which they were meant to have made a boat trip. But as it was pouring with rain their Chinese hosts had hastily arranged a tent and some food and local musicians to play and they said to the Australians that in China, when people get together, they dance!

'Everyone's faces fell,' said Tam. 'We were all cold and wet and miserable and no-one felt like dancing. But when something has been carefully planned and it goes wrong so the plans are changed and guests don't adapt and join in, I think it's boring and pathetic of them! So I got up and danced! Malcolm really hates dancing, so I grabbed somebody else and danced my heart out!'

Next day the Australian press reported: 'In Urum-chi, in the foothills of the snow-capped mountains along the Russian border, Mrs. Fraser joined in lively traditional dances, which delighted her hosts and re-vived the spirits of the tiring Australian party.'

Chapter 6
HAZARDS OF THE DAY

As novelist Jean Webster once wrote: 'Anyone can rise to a crisis and face a crushing tragedy with courage; but to meet the petty hazards of the day with a laugh— I really think that requires spirit.'

Life in The Lodge did assume a certain routine, however bizarre that routine might sound in comparison with most Australian households. The week really started on Tuesday because Parliament sat on Tuesday and that meant the PM would have to be back in Canberra. From Friday to Monday, when the House was not sitting, the Frasers might be found anywhere in Australia, Opening or Closing, Laying or Launching, Inspecting or Correcting.

On Tuesdays Tam would begin the day by organising the menus for the week with the chef at The Lodge. This could be quite a lengthy and complicated process depending on how busy their program was and whom they were entertaining in that week.

For instance, amongst other things, the Frasers instigated a weekly dinner for backbenchers (and their wives if they happened to be in Canberra). Tamie and Malcolm thought it would be a good idea to give each backbencher a chance to see The Lodge and chat to their PM in an informal atmosphere. These dinners Tam irreverently called Eat-It-And-Beat-Its because the guests only came at six and left at eight, between sittings of the House.

Next up she and her secretary, Susannah Law-Smith, tackled the correspondence, which was increasingly large and disparate. Each week there was a rash of problem letters from people who needed help in all sorts of areas, like social security or immigration, and who thought Tamie might be a soft touch.

'Some of them were heart-rending letters about how mum was stuck in Yugoslavia and we want her to come out,' Susannah told me. 'I don't know what people thought Tamie could do about it. Perhaps they felt they could appeal to her senses as a woman. Anyway she answered them all and forwarded their letters on to the appropriate Minister. She always followed them up, too, to see that they weren't lost in the system.'

Some of the letters Tamie received were quite extraordinary, and lightened her day. 'I remember one which arrived shortly after Tamie had made some comment in a magazine article about the benefits of breast feeding,' said Susannah. 'From the writing this letter appeared to be from an old lady and it said she was so glad the Prime Minister and Tamie did not believe the breast was for fondling but that it should be used for the purpose for which God intended, the feeding of infants! It was really worth framing,' said Susannah.

Each week Tamie also received a plethora of invitations. Trying to decide which to accept and which to refuse was always vexing. The school holidays were sacrosanct. They were kept free for the children. But for the rest of the year she endeavoured to attend at least two or three functions on her own each week. 'That mightn't sound much,' said Tam, 'but in fact it involved an awful lot of travelling—getting on a plane and flying to Sydney, then perhaps catching another plane and going on to Moree or Gosford, or flying to Brisbane and then going up to Mt Isa or going to Perth and then out to Meekatharra—day trips all the way.

'Most of the functions I attended involved old peoples' homes, kindergartens, retarded childrens' centres, women's refuges, schools for the blind, hospitals and factories,' she said. Luncheon invitations were innumerable. Tam could have gone to two lunches anywhere in Australia—every day she was in office, Susannah told me, and at most of these events she was required to make a speech.

Tamie always wrote her own speeches, 'because anything sensible written by a proper speech writer sounds all wrong coming out of my mouth. Occasionally if I had to speak on something technical I sought help from one of Malcolm's press officers or somebody in his office, but usually I could only use their contributions as a guide.'

This laissez-faire technique caused occasional problems. 'I remember once in Darwin when I was standing in for Malcolm because he was ill with some bug and I had to lay a time bottle in the new cathedral. I stood up there on the platform with this wad of typed pages in my hand and it was 110 in the waterbag and I read the first dozen pages or so very earnestly—then I stopped. "You don't want to hear me read all these figures and statistics and things, do you?" I said, licking my thumb and turning over page after page unread. "You don't want to hear all this. What it really means is that the Government is being very supportive: they're really trying to help. They want you to know they understand your difficulties and they're giving you some money. That's the real message. Now you know the rest without hearing all these endless figures coming out of my mouth which I know you won't listen to anyway, and it's damn hot in the sun, isn't it!" and they all smiled up at me and thought that was fine so I finished off with a bit more and it was all a great success.

'But when it came time to lay the stone, the cement was all sloppy and I had awful trouble with it. And I thought gosh, don't they know how to make cement in Darwin? But later on after the ceremony they told me that the concrete had been timed to reach just the right consistency in 20 minutes because Malcolm's speech was scheduled to last 20 minutes. When my version of it took only 10 minutes it threw everything into dissarray! It was jolly lucky the brass plaque didn't slide off the wall and land in a sloppy puddle at my feet!'

One great difficulty of organisation at The Lodge was dove-tailing Tamie's schedule in with the PM's, Susannah told me. 'All day they would both be off in different directions and we would have to get them back in time for dinner together,' said Susannah. 'Tamie received a lot of diplomatic calls, too. The wives of the heads of station would ring for an appointment. They would call to pay their respects and have a cup of tea and a pleasant chat.' Each visit would last for exactly 20 minutes and they all had to be fitted into the diary.

The concept of the role of Prime Minister's wife has always intrigued me. It is a job, yet not a job; demanding, yet totally undefined. One day when Tamie was home at Nareen and we had some time together, I said to her: 'What is a typical day for the wife of a PM?'

'There's no such thing!' she answered.

'Then what did you do on, say, last Wednesday, for example?'

'Oh, Wednesday!' she groaned. 'Yes, I'll tell you about Wednesday because it was a typical day. I left The Lodge at about six-thirty in the morning to catch the seven o'clock plane to Melbourne, which was the only one available. I landed in Melbourne and headed north, stopping on the way to visit some old friends to fill in time before arriving in Bendigo to be guest speaker at a Liberal luncheon for 300 people.'

'Heaven help them!' I said.

'Quite,' she replied unruffled. 'Then after lunch I had to do a television thing and visit another park and we were a bit behind schedule and racing for the plane when we got into an awful skid—there was some oil on the road or something, it wasn't the driver's fault—but we turned 180 degrees, narrowly missing a large white post, and ended up facing the way we'd come. No-one was hurt, but it used up even more adrenalin than making the speech!

'Anyway, we pressed on, more cautiously now, and arrived back at Tullamarine to find we'd just missed my plane. But luckily there was a VIP plane on the tarmac just taking off for Canberra, so I rushed over and hitched a ride on that. I finally got back to The Lodge at a quarter to six, flung on a dinner dress and a fresh face while I watched the TV headlines then raced downstairs to find all the Premiers assembled in the drawing-room, drinking tomato juice and glaring at one another.

'You could have cut the atmosphere with a knife!' said Tam. 'After their conference (an annual meeting to apportion the states' share of Commonwealth revenue) they were tense with each other and all furious with Malcolm. I waded in and tried to make bright conversation, but it was an uphill battle. We all sat down for dinner and they were still glaring at each other and speaking in monosyllables. I'd had a Big Day and I was suddenly *sick* of it. So I slapped the table with both hands, gave them all my widest smile, and said: "You were all marvellous on television tonight!"

'Well, they were stunned!' she said, 'I could see them thinking back, their minds going grind grind trying to remember back what they'd said. And they knew they'd all been beastly about Malcolm and they all had the grace to look slightly embarrassed at having accepted hospitality after being so vile—and then at last they saw the funny side of it and laughed, and everything was alright! But, since you ask—those are the kinds of situations you have to cope with on your average day as the PM's wife!'

Although Tam had to have a security guard with her whenever she attended any official engagements, she loved to zoom around Canberra on her own in her little blue car—number plate LUV-000, and known as the Lovebug. 'One day after returning to The Lodge from the summer holidays I was dashing out to have my hair done to make myself fit for public consumption again and I had on dark glasses and a scarf tied around my head.

'When I drove up to the gates of The Lodge the policeman on duty, instead of opening them to let me out, stopped my car, marched around to my window, and said: "Yes?"

"I would like to go out please."

"Where are you going?"

"I am going out!"

"You can't go out without permission."

"I am Mrs. Fraser! and I want to go out!"

"You can't be. She's been out all day."

"Officer, I'm very sorry, but you must have had the wrong animal!"

'I took off my scarf and dark glasses and said, "Is that better? Now, would you kindly open the gates of this prison, and let me *out*!" and away I sped in a shower of gravel.'

At The Lodge Tamie had to entertain a constant stream of visitors. 'Do you find it difficult making conversation to VIPs whom you've never met before?' I asked. 'What do you talk to them about?'

'It's hard to say—you try to think of things of mutual interest,' said Tam, rather vaguely.

'Is it ever a problem?' I persisted. 'Do you ever sit there thinking, what can I say next?'

'I always do that *before* I go out to dinner, either in Australia or travelling overseas. I think about what I can possibly say to people I've never met before. What sort of generalities I can safely probe, whether books or plays or a current world drama or something. I try to select a couple of topics and hope the other person will contribute something too.

'Invariably when Malcolm was in office, they didn't, because I was always sitting next to the person making the speech (this is in Australia) and they were always totally preoccupied with what they were going to say and couldn't have been less interested in talking to me. And that makes conversation very hard work! Of course some visitors don't speak English and you have to cope with the same situation through interpreters, which adds to the strain.'

'You have to remember that official visitors are travelling all the time to different countries and meeting different people, and the minute they hit the ground they're asked have you had a good flight? Have you been here before? How long is your stay in this country? It's all so *boring!* One day Mr. and Mrs. George Bush were arriving from America and I thought the poor dears, they've been to 10 countries in 10 days and probably had the same conversations at each place, so after Malcolm and I had said how-do-you-do at the airport, I said: Aunt Harriet loves arrivals but she hates departures! They looked at me a bit strangely so I said oh yes, and she loves meetings but hates conferences! It's a word game, you know?

'We all got into our cars to travel back from the airport and I said Aunt Harriet hates highways but she loves streets! She hates overtaking, but she loves passing! The visitors became intrigued, so when they arrived at The Lodge for dinner that night I carried it on—Aunt Harriet loves dinners but she hates lunches! I said. She loves business and simply adores commerce but she loathes trade! She hates reports but goes wild over submissions. The game continued on and off all night as more and more people caught on and joined in!

'And when the visitors left I had such a nice letter back saying how much everyone had enjoyed the night—it's been a bit different, a bit of *fun*, you know? And *fun* is a rare commodity in politics!'

Official entertaining and public engagements put a great strain on the wardrobe and I asked Tam how she coped with her clothes.

'Well, buying clothes becomes a chore rather than a pleasure because you have to go for things which will look suitable from eleven o'clock in the morning until after dinner at night. I mean, you leave home at seven a.m. and fly to Adelaide or Melbourne or somewhere, and first up there'll be a morning tea party, then there'll be a luncheon and then you'll be whisked off somewhere else to afternoon tea, followed by a drinks party and ending up with dinner at night—all in the same dress! I do believe,' she said thoughtfully,

'that you must try not to look how you often feel—
dog tired—so I learned to ask for half an hour to
myself before the evening session. A quick shower
always revives the spirit.

'I think my record for dressing is seven and a half
minutes from go to whoah for the Lord Mayor's Ball!
I'd had functions in Tasmania all that day and the
Governor General gave me a lift back to Melbourne
in his plane.

'I changed my make-up in the car on the way in
from the airport and then when I reached my mother-
in-law's flat in South Yarra, where we always stay, I
raced upstairs, threw off my day clothes, pulled on
my long dress, and while Amanda, my new Secretary,
did it up at the back, Anthony my hair-dresser attacked
my hair. When I arrived at the ball and looked around
at all the glittering and immaculate guests, I couldn't
help wondering how many of them had dressed in just
seven and a half minutes!'

Tamie had another all-time record quick change in
Canberra one day when Prince Charles was flying in.
'In order for us to arrive at the airport at precisely the
right time, we have to leave The Lodge at the same
moment as the Governor General leaves Yarralumla.
This enables the PM to arrive one minute before the
GG, as scheduled in the welcoming ceremony.

'For once in our lives Malcolm and I were ready,
sitting and having a cup of coffee and waiting for the
GG's telephone call to speed us on our way. On the
coffee tray there was a plate of chocolate biscuits and
Droopy, our springer spaniel, smelt them, looked
longingly at them, started to drool, and just as the
telephone rang put his chin on my lap leaving a huge
wet patch of slobber all over the front of my freshly
cleaned pale-beige suit!

'I rushed back up to the bedroom, grabbed something else, then flew down the stairs again, re-dressing
as I came. There were various security guards and
members of staff standing around the front hall and
I cried: "Please avert your gaze—this is *an emergency!*" and I was still pulling on my jacket as we got
into the car and drove off!

'You see, I think clothes are important,' said Tam. 'I try to look presentable always—ever since one day just after Malcolm became Leader of the Opposition and Eda called in to see me at Fairlie Court just as I was leaving to go shopping. "Tam, you just can't go out like that!" she said, "you look awful! You can't look that awful anymore!" and that made me aware that now I have a responsibility to look tidy—out of respect for the position.

'I always wear Australian clothes and have to choose clothes which will wash easily and not crush and all those boring, sensible things. Same with my hair. I have to wear a style that can cope with both the windy tarmac and the white tie on the same evening. I tell you, dressing for politics, like politics itself, is only the art of the possible!'

'Was it ever impossible?' I asked.

'Only once!' she said, 'It was a long time ago when we were going back to Canberra at the end of one school holidays and the children were very small. I had a baby, a 3, 6 and 7 year old to dress and breakfast, and as our flight left at 7am I thought an excellent idea would be to pack nearly everything the night before and send all the suitcases on out to the aiport, leaving just a change of clothes for the next day.

'But in the morning when I came to dress I found I had no shoes. None! Every single pair was packed and out at the airport! All I had to wear were some terrible old jiffies which I'd put on to tidy the flat! It was certainly too early to buy another pair, so I went to the medicine cupboard and took out some old bandages and bound up one leg and one ankle and pulled the old jiffies on over the top.

'Then I gathered up the children and limped off to the airport, muttering something about a ski-ing accident! The children were ultra solicitous and I thought I was being most convincing but after we'd been there about ten minutes, Malcolm said: "Go easy, Tam, you're over-acting! You're over-doing it, old girl, you're over-doing it!" It was neither the first time nor the last in my political experience he was to say that!'

Chapter 7
FIRE ON TWO FRONTS

For the Frasers, 1977 was an exacting year. It began with a disaster in their electorate and ended with near electoral disaster. The months between encompassed the full spectrum of political experience and illustrate the diversity of demands placed upon the wife of a PM.

Tamie and Malcolm returned to Canberra from Nareen in early February and were just gearing up for the new parliamentary year when a searing north wind sent a series of bushfires raging through parts of western Victoria, including large areas of Wannon. The losses were appalling.

'I'd been out of Canberra all day,' said Tam, 'and arrived back about dinner time to hear the news. We both felt sick. Lives had been lost and many homes destroyed.' The tiny township of Streatham had been decimated and in many separate fires that day huge areas of countryside were desperately badly burned—including a major slice of our parents' property, Nareeb Nareeb.

Tamie wanted to jump on a plane and fly down then and there to be with them, but she knew that was impossible. 'Arrangements had to be made in Canberra and, anyway, the middle of the night isn't the time to go barging in and trying to help—you'd only be a nuisance. So from eleven o'clock that night, when the staff disappeared from the kitchen, until three in the morning, I made shortbread! That was the only recipe I could remember! Because at fires all country women make something—casseroles, cakes, soups and sandwiches, scones by the ute load to feed the fire-fighters and the families who have been burnt out, so I felt I just had to make something, I couldn't think of anything else to do.'

Malcolm and Tamie flew down to Victoria first thing next morning. They drove straight to the townships of Cressy and Streatham, south west of Ballarat, which were the hardest hit. 'But it's difficult to know how to be of any help,' said Tam.

'We moved around and talked to a lot of people, visited Red Cross centres and Emergency Service Centres which cope with feeding and clothing people and housing them. It was heart-rending. The people were numb with shock. And what can you say? You can't just go on saying how sorry you are, and you wonder if you're just getting in the damn way, or is it a help and comfort for people to see your concern? It's a hard thing to get right.

'Those fires were particularly sad because they came at the end of years and years of poor seasons and then the first really good spring. There was feed every-where, long grass and thick stubbles, and everyone had been saying, "Hey, look at this country! Isn't it looking great?" Then suddenly—it's all gone. Burnt out *because* of all the grass. You could see the deso-lation on people's faces—how are we going to climb out of debt now?

'One woman I spoke to had lost everything and I'll never forget what she said: "I was lying on the floor covered with a blanket, spread-eagled over my three children, my husband was out somewhere, I didn't know where but I hoped to God he was safe, and the glass was melting around me and the fire was crackling and roaring and I knew at that moment and forever that the *only* thing in life is—*life*!"'

The Frasers drove through miles of blackened land-scape littered with the bodies of burnt animals, twisted fence lines and piles of smouldering rubble. They reached Nareeb Nareeb about lunchtime. Eda and I

were there already and so glad to see them. Our parents
had not yet had time to stop and take stock of the
situation, but they both seemed numb and shaken. It
was the third fire that had burned through Nareeb
Nareeb and this time the experience had somehow
aged them. For a day at least, Grannie and Grandfather
seemed only just In Charge.

But on this occasion the homestead and buildings
had survived intact and now my brother Hugh and
his wife Frankie were there to gather up the pieces and
face the task of rebuilding the Merino stud once more.

Lunch that day was soup and sandwiches served in
the shearers' huts by a team of women who materi-
alised from somewhere with armfuls of bread and cold
meat to feed the army of men who had appeared out
of the blue to help with rounding up the surviving
stock and shooting those which had been too badly
burned to recover. Chris and Robin Ritchie, Eda's
husband, were among them. Frankie was in charge of
the production line and while Eda and I sliced and
spread, Tamie stood at an old wooden trestle table for
two hours serving cups of tea. Malcolm had gone on
alone to visit other centres nearby and at about four
he returned to collect her and go on back to Canberra.

I will never forget Tam's face that day as she drove
away. Her anguish at having to leave the family at
such a time was palpable but she said nothing, just
smiled and hugged us all and climbed into the back
of the white Commonwealth car. As it rolled away
up the drive she turned and waved goodbye, still smiling. But I was standing close by and I could see the
tears that were streaming down her face.

In March, 1977, the Queen and the Duke of Edin-
burgh came to Australia for three weeks' tour and
Don Chipp resigned from the Liberal Party. Most of
what I learned about either event came from avid scan-
ning of television and newspapers. Tamie didn't want
to talk about Don Chipp and wasn't prepared to talk
about the Queen. She observed the propriety of never
revealing a royal conversation to a taunting degree,
and no amount of sisterly cajoling or cross-examina-

tion ever broke down her reserve on the subject.

In April Malcolm was battling with the premiers to put in place voluntary wage-price restraints for three months, so Tamie had to fly off to Germany alone to launch a ship. 'I was asked to launch the last of the Australian National Line cargo ships which was called "Australian Progress", a bulk carrier of 138,000 tonnes,' she said. 'Susannah Law-Smith and I went to Hamburg for a week. The launching coincided with the centenary of the Blohm & Voss shipyards so it was all rather a Big Deal.

'The day was freezing cold with a bitter wind and when we arrived at the shipyards there was a huge crowd in attendance. Herr Dr. Werner Bartels, the chairman of Blohm & Voss led me up some steps on to a dais erected beside the hull of the ship. Its bow towered above me like a four-storey building.

'Helmut Schmidt stood up in his pit workers hat and made an address to the workers, obviously election rally stuff, shouting and shouting and pounding the lectern, whipping up the crowd. Susannah thought it was really spine-chilling. To her it sounded just like the re-run of a thirties' movie. We listened to it all through a female interpreter, and I found it disconcerting to hear Schmidt's words coming from the mouth of a woman. It's somehow harder to comprehend and believe what you're hearing if it's being presented in a voice of the opposite sex.'

Tam had never forgotten once seeing a cartoon of a great and mighty ocean liner, the *S.S. Oh, Blast!*, so-called because the woman who named her had slipped at the vital moment. 'So when my big moment came I stepped forward very, very carefully, and said: "I name this ship the 'Australian Progress'! May God Bless her—and all who sail in her!" Then I cut the string and a bottle of champagne went *sploosh* against the side of the hull and the ship slid slowly down into the water while all the workers, all the men who had built her, cheered wildly. It was very moving—this huge inanimate object slowly coming to life.'

That night Blohm & Voss gave a dinner at the Hamburg Congress Centre. There were 900 guests. Tamie was asked to make an address. 'Of course she did it brilliantly,' Susannah told me, 'but at some cost. Tamie used to say she lost weight whenever she had to make a speech—all that adrenalin racing around—and that's what kept her thin. Well, she must have lost pounds and pounds in Hamburg that night!'

Tamie and Susannah arrived back in Sydney at 6 am on Good Friday morning, 'and Malcolm had all the children out at the airport to greet me!' Tam said. 'It was Easter holidays and there they were at 6 am bright-eyed and beaming with What Are We Going To Do Today, Mum? written all over their faces! Now I hadn't been to bed since Tuesday, but I was so thrilled to see them that I took a deep breath and said how about the Zoo? This was greeted by wild cheers of approval, so we all went to Toronga Park and if by the end of the day I was walking around like a mechanical robot, nobody seemed to notice!'

In June the Frasers flew to london to attend the Queen's Silver Jubilee Celebrations.

'What really struck me was the enormous upsurge of feeling for the monarchy in England at that time and how everyone suddenly looked at the Queen and saw what she had done for 25 years.

'This realisation was reflected all over England. Wherever we went each tiny town and hamlet had Jubilee celebrations organised and something royal on display, whether it were red-white-and-blue petunias growing in their window boxes or flags flying in their gardens, or on their cars or at their playing fields. The usual British reserve had been abandoned and the whole country was proudly and overtly royalist.'

On Wednesday, June 8, the day after they attended the Queen's Jubilee Service at St. Paul's Cathedral Malcolm attended the opening session of the Commonwealth Heads of Government Conference at Lancaster House. The Conference was attended by the leaders of 33 Commonwealth nations and ran for eight days. It was chaired by the British Prime Minister, James Callaghan, and included a weekend retreat at a hotel in Scotland called Gleneagles, which gave its name to the agreement thrashed out there between Commonwealth leaders on sporting ties with South Africa.

'We arrived at Gleneagles on Saturday afternoon and being a golfer I just had to take to the fairways!' Tam told me. 'It was drizzling rain and the other wives thought I was mad so I had to play by myself. My caddie was a grand old Scot with a leathery weather-beaten face, quite ageless, who had obviously caddied there for years and knew every trap and pitfall of the course.

'There were three courses there actually and I played the King's course, which had beautiful velvet fairways and hideous awful gorse down each side just waiting to ensnare your ball if you went off the straight and narrow.

'It also ensnared the poor security men who were hiding in it to protect any golfing PMs. The security men popped out of the gorse and waved and cheered everytime I fluffed a shot and remained deeply hidden everytime I did a cracker—which annoyed me monumentally! All the holes had names, and there was one short hole with bunkers all around the green known as Carter's Teeth!

'When I came in from my round of golf I found the HOG's (Heads of Government) all sitting around in little groups, corralled in different parts of the hotel lounge, sort of talking conspiratorially. There were four or five PMs in one corner and two or three in another corner and some more somewhere else, and you could have cut the atmosphere with a knife. There was a real feeling of something going on.

'Malcolm was quietly playing musical chairs from group to group. He believed it was terribly important that the Africans didn't become polarized against the rest of the Commonwealth over the issue of sporting ties with South Africa. He had his first brush with Muldoon over it. Muldoon was dead against the agreement and being a real pain.

'But one thing I think Malcolm is good at,' Tam

went on, 'is understanding peoples' ideological limits: understanding that you can't expect people of one ideology to go beyond a certain point, as you can with another. And yet there is always a grey area and I think he's good at sifting that out and perhaps describing it in a logical way to people, so they can see that they are not betraying their own beliefs by giving a little here or there.

'That Gleneagles Agreement was very delicately balanced. It wasn't as far as some of the Africans wanted to go and it was further than the New Zealanders liked, yet all managed to live with it. Malcolm was a moving force in achieving that agreement.'

After the Frasers returned from their London trip Susannah Law-Smith left her position as Tamie's secretary to be married. Tam was thrilled for Susannah, but most upset to see her go. She appointed Amanda Derham in her place and was relieved when Amanda quickly assumed Susannah's role not only of efficient secretary but of friend and ally as well.

One of Amanda's first jobs as new secretary was to review Tamie's program and she found it groaning with overload. 'You don't mean to become so booked up,' Tam tried to explain, 'but you accept an invitation for six months in advance because from that distance your itinerary looks clear, then in the meantime other engagements arise and the whole thing snowballs so that you end up living in a state of panic; what our driver always called "permanent organised panic"!'

And between the stream of official engagements her diaries were interspersed with: Phoebe—dentist; Angela—haircut; Hugh—parent/teacher interview. The children, though out of sight, were never out of mind.

'Did Tamie tell you how she managed to squeeze in a game of golf one day?', a back bench wife and a good friend of Tam's asked me one day. 'Tamie had a ladies' luncheon organised at The Lodge and she badly wanted 18 holes before she was due at an embassy function that evening. So we decided to work out a plan to help us get to the golf course in good time. At about 2.15 Tamie gave me the nod and I stood up and said, "Goodness! Look at the time! I simply must fly! Would anyone like a lift?" Well that was a failure because they all had their own cars, so I said all my goodbyes rather noisily and swept out the front door—then quickly slipped around to the back of The Lodge.

'I found a man sweeping the garage out the back and I asked him please could he direct me to the fire-escape. He looked at me very strangely, but concurred and I flew up the stairs through the back bedrooms and waited breathless on the landing while Tamie said goodbye, so sorry you have to go! to all the wives. Then off we dashed for a quick round of golf. And I'm glad we did. I think it did her the world of good.'

But my mother used to ring and say: 'Tamie darling, you're doing Far Too Much. It will take its toll!' and she was right. One day during a particularly busy week Tam attended an agricultural show in country New South Wales with her secretary, Amanda Derham. She judged the Miss Tiny Tot competition and presented the prize for the best trade display and then one of the stewards of the local P & A Society showed her around the exhibits. 'And I couldn't work out why Mrs. Fraser was being so slow!' said Amanda. 'She was taking forever and I didn't like to push her in case she was really interested, but I was wanting to hurry her up because we had a very tight schedule that day and I was meant to be timing it all.

"She was studying each exhibit carefully and saying all the right things like How interesting! and Oh really! and Is that so? but she was as white as a sheet and her eyes looked glazed and she was being so slow! We finally finished the exhibits and said our farewells and when we got back to the car I said "I'm really sorry if I was hurrying you but I was worried about the time, are you alright?", and she put her hand over her eyes, and said: "No. I'm feeling absolutely bloody. It's another migraine. Please take me home."'

Although inflation was down, unemployment was running at 5.4% and the government was under constant pressure from opposition and press. Malcolm was working long hours, absorbed with budget issues and with framing legislation for the approval for uranium mining.

As David Barnett, his Press Secretary, was to write of him later: 'He was a decision-making machine. He ate up his paper, brief case after brief case, on planes, in cars, at home or on the farm, in the office late at night, when appointments were over and the rest of Australia had turned off the telly and gone to bed.'

Meanwhile work had begun under the direction of the Official Establishments Trust on renovations to the staff quarters of The Lodge, and on August 21 the Minister Assisting the Prime Minister, Tony Staley, announced the formation of the Australia Fund 'to allow the public to participate directly, through donations of cash and works of art, including furnishings, in the fitting out of Government House, Kirribilli, Admiralty House and The Lodge.'

This was Tamie's brainchild and she was delighted but there was no time to get it off the ground before Malcolm, after fierce and prolonged press speculation, called a federal election for December 10, twelve months ahead of time.

Then the fat hit the fire. The federal Treasurer, Phillip Lynch, was forced to resign over alleged land dealings. Although he was subsequently cleared of all impropriety the affair was a gift to the opposition and the press and caused great personal distress to both the Frasers and the Lynch's, and electorally the incident could not have occurred at a worse time.

A by-election in the Victorian seat of Greensborough showed a swing to Labor of 6.35%. In the Queensland state election which followed there was a 7.3% swing to Labor. 'The situation was really grim,' said Tam, 'and for the last two weeks, at least, before the campaign began we hadn't been to bed before 4 am.'

It showed. I saw Tamie and Malcolm when they came to Hamilton on November 21 to launch the Liberal Party campaign in their electorate before flying

Malcolm Fraser, the youngest Australian M.P. at the time, weds Tamara Beggs in 1956.

As election tension mounts Tamie Fraser watches her husband answer questions after leaving the Dandenong Octoberfest on November 15 1975.

Tamie and the family's dogs at Nareen.

The Fraser family at home in 1975. The children (from left) are Angela, Mark, Hugh and Phoebe.

A confident Prime Minister and his wife on August 30, 1976.

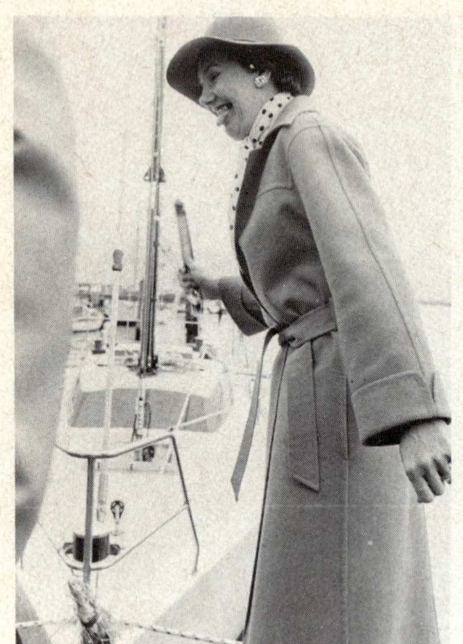

The family Christmas, 1977. Back row: Robin Ritchie, Hugh Beggs, Frankie Beggs, Chris Hindhaugh, Malcolm Fraser, Hugh Fraser (hidden), Mark Fraser. Middle row: Mrs. Una Fraser, David Beggs, Eda Ritchie, Phoebe Fraser, Tamie Fraser, the author, James Hindhaugh, Mrs. and Mr. Sandford Beggs. Front row: Angela Fraser, Eda Hindhaugh, Skye Ritchie, Daniel Ritchie, Jason Ritchie, Richard Beggs, Julia Hindhaugh, Sally Beggs.

Opposite Left:
A difficult berth as Tamara Fraser christens the yacht Pioneer Sound, *Australian Challenger for the World One Ton Cup in 1977.*

Opposite Right:
'I feel like foreman material,' jokes Tamie Fraser as she gets ready to lay the foundation stone at a new wing of the Austin Hospital, Melbourne in 1976.

Opening The Lodge has its complications.

Prime Minister's study at The Lodge.

Tamie Fraser talks with some Aboriginal children on a visit to the Northern Territory in 1978.

The Frasers and their party visit the Sanzen-in Temple during their visit to Japan in 1979.

Tamie Fraser dances with President Gerald Ford in the East Room of the White House during the Fraser's visit to the U.S. in 1976.

Angela Fraser joins her mother in looking at photographs of the U.S. visit.

on to Melbourne for the big nationally televised rally in the Malvern Town Hall that night. Malcolm looked grey and his eyes had receded back beneath his eyebrows as they always did when he was exhausted. Tamie was bright but taut, strung up tighter than a violin.

When they arrived in Hamilton just before lunchtime they were advised by an airport official that their son, Mark, had been trying to contact them from Deniliquin all morning. Malcolm went straight to the 'phone.

'Dad, the ute's blown up!' Mark told him, and described how the temperature light had come on and the engine seized, &c, &c. Standing behind Malcolm in the 'phone booth Tamie could gather both ends of the conversation and she knew from the tension in Malcolm's shoulders what was flashing through his mind: surely to God the ute can wait! . . . click . . . click a ute is terribly important to a jackaroo and Mark is asking for help . . .

'Mark, write this down,' Tamie heard him say as he took a deep breath. 'I want the exact details on what is the problem, what new parts are needed and how much it will cost to fix. Plus a valuation on the ute as it is—from at least two different dealers. Got that?'

'Yes, Dad.'

'Right then. Now I've got to go and launch an election. But I'll ring you back as soon as I can.' Which he did, Tamie told me, the moment they landed in Melbourne about five that afternoon. And over the next few days, ringing from hotel lobbies, airport lounges and street 'phone booths all over the country, Malcolm sorted out the problem of Mark's ute with the same controlled thoroughness that he was at the same time dissecting Gough Whitlam's policy speech and hammering the electorate with the need for a coalition victory.

As the campaign progressed there were some noisy and even violent demonstrations. 'After a while you learned to sense the difference,' said Tam, 'pick out what were just rowdy, unruly crowds and what was rent-a-mob violence; in some cases controlled, manipulated violence. Probably the nastiest demonstration we experienced in that campaign, the one I resented most because it was *SO* outrageous, was the one at the Northcote Hospice Centre. This was a centre for the terminally ill, to try to help people come to terms with facing death. They were cancer patients or heart patients, for instance, with very limited futures.

'A service was held in the church and all these patients in wheel chairs had to be hustled in and out through a mob of demonstrators throwing cans and rotten fruit and refuse and shrieking abuse. I'll never forget the faces of those poor people, they were terrified, helpless in their wheelchairs in the midst of this screaming mob. I was not so much afraid that day as terribly, terribly angry.

'Because of the sort of place it was, the police had not been expecting trouble and there were not enough of them there to control the situation. I got a rotten egg right between my shoulder blades in my favourite suit. I only wish I'd worn the dress which I wore for a meeting at Monash University the night before. The dress was new, but I hated it and I thought, well, if it's damaged at least I'll be able to throw it out! But the police were at Monash in force and the situation never got out of hand like it did at Northcote.

'I think what frightened me more than anything else about the violence we suffered in elections was that it was intentional—set up beforehand. That Northcote demonstration was organised from the office of a Melbourne Labor MP—it was all in the papers—but it resulted in such a terrific electoral backlash that the word went out to pull out the goons, and after that we had no violence in any of the following elections.'

On Thursday December 1, nine days before polling day, an Age poll listed unemployment as the main issue of the election, followed some distance behind by inflation and the ability to manage the economy. Gough Whitlam and the Labor Party honed in on these issues but Malcolm was off and away campaigning on tax cuts and that issue was not even on the list.

Slowly the tide began to turn. Opinion polls revealed a return of support to the government. The Frasers campaigned even harder, racing around Australia in a finely-controlled frenzy of rallies and rhetoric. 'Elections are times when the air is filled with speeches—and vice versa, eh Mal?' said brother Hugh one day as they raced through Nareeb Nareeb. Too true! But at the close of counting on December 10 the Coalition had won another huge majority, 48 seats, the second biggest landslide in Australian political history. Back to Canberra and back to work. The show was still firmly on the road.

Chapter 8
LIFE IN CANBERRA

One day not long ago I heard an eminent Australian asked in a radio interview what, in her opinion, was the worst decision made by any Commonwealth government since Federation. Without hesitation she answered: 'Canberra!'

'Canberra's always been bashed,' said Tam, when I asked her opinion. 'I'm sure it will become a great city, but at present it's probably a bit limited. People tend to scratch each other's backs. Having no industry or commerce makes it rather a narrow society. It's no-one's fault, just a result of the setup.

'Canberra is very stratified. People with a certain income live in one area and people with another income live in another area. In the capital cities you have a much greater variation of living standards and life-styles all mixed in together. In Canberra everything is the same price range and nothing must be below a certain standard in a certain area and everyone knows what everyone's house is worth. I think that's bad, a bad concept in the beginning—too structured.'

When Tamie first came to Canberra as a young bride in 1957 everyone she met had a bald head. 'I spent my 21st birthday walking around the War Memorial in tears because everyone I met in Canberra was so *old!* Looking back I suppose they were all around 40 at the time. Then Doug Anthony's father resigned and Doug became the member for Richmond. Malcolm came home from the House one night and said he'd met young Doug and he seemed a good sort of bloke.

His wife Margot was coming up next week. Why not ask them to have dinner with us?

'We arranged to meet on the top of the steps in King's Hall at 6.15—and I can still remember the battle I had that night trying to squeeze into a pretty dinner dress when I was four months pregnant. I squeezed and shoved and rolled around the floor trying to do up the zip, but it was hopeless and I was forced to wear my first maternity outfit, which in those days was a sort of full top falling over a tight skirt underneath. And when we got to Parliament House there was Margot Anthony in exactly the same rig and looking equally embarrassed. We have been firm friends ever since! She had her first son just ahead of me— beating me by three days!

'A few months later Malcolm took Margot and me shopping at the brand new Bailey Arcade in Civic,' Tam continued. 'Doug was away, and Margot and I were both pretty bulgy by that stage. As we walked along we passed a group of youths and they gazed up at Malcolm, so big and tall, with an enormous pregnant woman on each arm. One of the youths turned to the others, and said: "Wow! Did you guys see that? Gives you an inferiority complex, doesn't it!" '

In 1957 the federal government under Robert Menzies established the National Capital Development Commission to complete the establishment of Canberra as a seat of government. 'At that time Canberra was still just a sprawling country town with some dairy farms in the middle of it and a river running through,' said Tam. 'And it was country town in atmosphere, too. Because of the hours which Parliament sat everyone had dinner between six and eight o'clock at night.

'I often used to meet Malcolm in Parliament House and dine with him there, then go on home. And as I went home I used to notice that all the lights in the streets were turned out. It might be only 8.30 at night but there were no lights left on anywhere! No television, you see, and everyone just went to bed. And when you walked around Canberra in the daytime you noticed that every woman was pregnant! There was simply nothing else to do!'

After two years in a rented house the Frasers built a house in Canberra, at Daly Street in Deakin. 'People said we were committing political suicide to live away from the electorate because Wannon was a swinging seat, but we wanted to keep the family together, so moved up and down from Nareen every few months.

I find listening to parliament today is often a distasteful and disillusioning experience and I asked Tam if she thought that personal vilification and abuse had become worse over the years. 'It's always been pretty bad,' she told me, 'and members were just as rude to each other then as they are now, but they were rude and ribald rather than rude and vicious, as they are today. And there was more tolerance outside the House then, a feeling of you barrack for your footy team and I barrack for mine, and that's fine.

'There weren't the personal vendettas—although Eddie Ward had a personal vendetta against Mr. Menzies—but there was less of it, and I put this down to the fact that in those days people from both sides of the House talked to each other more. There was more cross-pollination between parties—or between groups within the same party, and I think this was due to the fact that there were then only three places in Parliament House where you could go; the House, the Party room (which was used as an office by 20 or so members because there wasn't any other space), or the Bar.

'So you were constantly meeting and talking with a range of different people.

'Nowadays members have 'fridges in their private rooms, and I think it has made Parliament very cliquey. Everyone has their own little coterie of friends who like to meet regularly, and you can't get more than 10 people into those tiny offices. In those early days everyone went to the Bar and you talked to lots more people, members of the Opposition as well, the ones you liked. There are ones you like and ones you don't like in either party. So it mixed everyone up and created a better overall atmosphere.'

Malcolm agreed. 'And not only are the debates more unpleasant now, but I think a lot of them are bad debates. Too many people read their speeches nowadays. It was against standing orders to read your speech when I first went into Parliament. You had notes, but you weren't meant to read.'

But the members' demeanor in the House has always been the same. 'I remember being absolutely shocked,' said Tam, 'the first time I went to watch a debate from the Visitors' Gallery! The Speaker sat in his chair looking quite magnificent in wig and gown and the heavy gold mace was gleaming on the Table, the Clerks of the House were there too and the Sergeant-At-Arms.

'It was all very proper and impressive—except for the Honourable Members who were all lounging around on their beautiful green leather seats, chatting to each other when someone was trying to speak, nibbling chocolates, reading newspapers or magazines. Some of them were even asleep! I thought it was appalling behaviour!' said Tam. 'I wouldn't want any school children to see this! I thought to myself— at the ripe old age of 21!

'When I came to Canberra in 1957 there were still a lot of MP's in the House who had come in in '49 at a time of a great political crisis like the one we had in '75, and it created much the same feeling,' Tam went on. 'Nowadays people tend to think of Sir Robert Menzies' leadership as always rock-solid and unchallenged.

'But I remember constant backbench rumbles and Malcolm being lobbied, would he support Dick Casey or Harold Holt if there was a spill? And looking back it's interesting to note that those rumbles were taking place roughly seven years after Mr. Menzies came to power, and Malcolm started having leadership problems with Andrew Peacock and so forth roughly seven years after he came to power.

There were some marvellous characters then, too, just as there are today. Arthur Caldwell had a tremendous wit. Eddie Ward spoke faster than any man I've ever heard, yet you could hear and understand him perfectly anywhere in the Chamber. Not to mention "Trombone" Thompson, whom you could hear and understand perfectly anywhere in Australia!

'Another marvellous character I remember was Bert James from Wollongong,' said Tam. 'One night, when proceedings were being broadcast, he stopped in the middle of his speech to the House, and said: "Hey, Joe Smith! (or whatever was the name of his dentist) Gidday there! I'll be over to collect my new set next Wednesday at three. I hope you're listening, and make sure you have 'em ready!" '

Tam told me another story about that era of a member of Parliament called Malcolm McKay who had been a prisoner of war in Colditz in Germany during the Second World War and had escaped and stowed away on a Swedish freighter. When the ship was safely out of German territorial waters this man had given himself up to the Captain. The Captain promptly turned the ship around and took him back to Germany. But he survived the war and years later attended a diplomatic reception at the Swedish Embassy in Canberra only to find himself once again face-to-face with that Captain—he was the new Swedish Ambassador!

'And this was a thing none of my generation could understand, this feeling of having real enemies,' said Tam. 'Perhaps the boys who fought in Vietnam and Korea have it, but most of my era really don't understand what people go on living through and keep having to face, like that Colditz prisoner, for the rest of their lives.'

Another situation arose in Parliament at that time which impressed Tamie with the same feeling. The Japanese Prime Minister, Mr. Kishi, was coming to Australia for the first official visit since the war, and a reception was to be held in his honour. 'I'll never forget the agonising that went on in the Parliament night after night, dinner table after dinner table, until three o'clock in the morning over that reception for the Japanese PM; all the members sitting around saying should we go, or shouldn't we? Will we, or won't we?'

'It was a question of not knowing the right thing to do. If you didn't go, were you being disloyal to the people who were trying to make a fresh start, because after all the war was over and life had to go on? If you did go, were you being disloyal to those who had suffered terribly as prisoners of the Japanese or even lost their lives?

'In the end we all went,' said Tam. 'And do you know who made the decision to go and who led us all in? Sir Wilfred Kent-Hughes and Sir Alexander Downer, both of whom had been prisoners of the Japanese. They were the leaders in making the point that we all have to live in the same world and look to the future and therefore we should all welcome Mr. Kishi to Canberra.'

I asked Tam how often she used to go to the House to listen to proceedings. 'I enjoyed question time or a good debate,' she said, 'but when the children were small it was hard to get away. And later on when Malcolm became PM there was seldom the time. I always tried to be there if there was some crisis on, something upsetting like a Minister resigning. But so much of parliament is just a function of passing endless legislation and was generally pretty monotonous.'

I had to agree. Tam used to take Eda and me to listen to proceedings in the House whenever we came to stay with her in Canberra. On our first visit we sat through the annual report of the Apple and Pear Board, and on our next the third reading of the Repatriation Allocations Bill. We did not find it riveting.

But occasionally the wits of the House, of which there were many, lightened the proceedings. Tam was in the House one night listening to a debate which followed a visit Prime Minister Harold Holt had made to the United States to meet President Lyndon Johnson. The Labor Party was castigating Mr. Holt for being too acceptingly pro-American, and for evidence they quoted his famous remark: 'All the way with LBJ!' 'It's better than "Half way in with Ho Chi Minh!" ' yelled some wag from the backbenches, and the House was in uproar.

'There was one prominent member of the Labor Party in those early days who used to gesticulate wildly when he made a speech,' said Tam. 'One night I was sitting in the Visitors' Gallery bored to the back axles and this MP got up to make a speech to an almost empty House. As he spoke he started shaking his fist in the air with the emotion of what he was saying and as it was after midnight and no-one else was there I shook my fist back at him in imitation. He noticed me doing it and stopped immediately. But after a few minutes he forgot and started shaking his fist again, it was just an automatic gesture, so I shook mine back and he became frightfully flustered and embarrassed and lost the whole thread of his speech! On dear! I was very young in those days. He was kind enough to laugh about the incident in later years.

'But it's amazing how the wheel turns full circle and all your sins come back to haunt you. For instance, the Commonwealth on occasion gives dinners at Parliament House and all members of the House of Reps. and senators are invited. These dinners are held in the Parliamentary diningroom which isn't big enough to accommodate everyone and so a number of back-benchers and their wives have to sit out in the wings.

'Mirrors are set up so that in theory the guests out there can watch the proceedings, but in reality all you can ever see is the guest speaker's right elbow or perhaps the back of his ear. So you are very tempted if the speaker is not interesting to carry on your own party and simply ignore the formalities of the evening.

'We spent years and years of parliamentary dinners out there in the wings when Malcolm was a back bencher so when we eventually made it to the High Table we knew exactly what was going on around the corner in the wings! We were sympathetic, but at the same time wished everyone out there would shut up and behave themselves!

'The same thing happened with protocol,' said Tam. 'I used to send it up in the early days and make fun of it, the rigid structure, the inflexibility. But when Malcolm became Minister for the Army and we suddenly had to arrive at places at 10.27 or 12.53, though it seemed ridiculous, I soon realised that if you didn't arrive precisely then you mucked the whole thing up; that it wasn't amusing to be late or be early. It's the only way a function can be smooth and well-run, if everyone tows the line and co-operates. I gradually learned to behave and do exactly as I was told—which was quite a drastic personality change for me!'

'But in the early days it nearly drove me mad! I'll never forget when I first came to Canberra as a young bride Malcolm and I went to dinner one night at an Ambassador's residence. All the other guests there, ambassadors' wives and so forth, were all decades older than me, and when we ladies left the table and withdrew upstairs, all the women stood around in groups telling stories about their grand-children.

'I didn't even have children at that stage, so while they were all talking I could see the loo was empty, and in I popped. And would you believe, I was ticked off soundly later on by a senior Australian diplomat's wife for going to the lavatory out of turn, out of the diplomatic order of precedence which official protocol demanded!

'I was told I should have waited until the end, until everyone else had been! I said to this wife, but that's ridiculous! I was busting and they were all talking and the loo was empty! And she said, "Well, please don't ever do it again. You've let your country down."

'In Canberra, if you are seated on the right of your host, it's your job to leave first, and no-one else can leave until you've gone,' she continued. 'At an embassy dinner one night in those early years I found myself seated on the left of the host which seemed quite safe, but what I didn't know was that the person on the right of the host was staying in the house.

'After dinner we all had coffee and then we sat and we sat and we sat and I thought, surely it's time to go home! When are they going to leave? Meanwhile one of the diplomatic wives (the same one as before!) was making faces at me across the room, but in those days I didn't have contact lenses and I couldn't make out what she was trying to tell me. I just sat there, weakly grinning back. The night wore on and on, and in the end our host rose to his feet and opened the doors, and we all left together. And I was in disgrace again!

'But really, I was so clearly too young and out of my depth that I think the diplomatic wife could have taken the lead and said "Shall we all go now?" and rescued me. But she was so tied up by protocol that she wouldn't dare step out of line, even to save a situation like that. I thought it was very peculiar, the whole thing,' said Tam. 'But I've had trouble following a disciplined line all my life!'

Although Tamie became the wife of the Prime Minister she had served a long apprenticeship as the wife of a backbencher and she knew the difficulties and frustrations—and often the loneliness—of that role.

'Something I started up quite soon after Malcolm became PM was a Women's Room in Parliament House (or a spouses' room, really, I suppose). Most politicians' wives make a great effort to come to Canberra to be with their husbands for a week or so. He wants you very much to come, but then you find he's terribly busy. He has committee meetings before the House sits, committee meetings often at mealtimes and you wonder why the hell you are here?

'You go around to talk to him during the House sittings when he might not be in the Chamber. His secretary looks down her nose at you, or his press secretary trips over your foot and curses. The offices are tiny and you're in the damn way and you feel completely de trop, out of place and a nuisance. And that makes you edgy which makes him edgy and instead of having a pleasant, companiable time together, the whole things ends up as a great strain!'

Tam felt that if there was a room in Parliament House set aside for spouses, somewhere for them to go to write a letter, watch television, or just make themselves a cup of coffee and read a book, it would be a valuable place for them to have.

'But I had a terrible job getting it,' she said. 'They kept saying there was nowhere, and I said there must be somewhere, and they all said it was a great idea but quite impossible. Finally Malcolm put his foot down and said Find Something! and it was amazing how quickly it happened and how much it is used.

'We had a book in there where wives could leave their names and messages about their whereabouts and plans. It meant you could contact people who would like some company too, perhaps lunch together, a bit of companionship while the members were busy. Its useful if wives can get together to have a bit of a whinge and get it out of their systems.

'Businessmens' wives are under pressure and on their own a lot too, but political wives have to contend with the publicity as well, and often on their own. It's wonderfully therapeutic to talk to someone who's in the same situation, someone you can dig in the ribs, and say, couldn't you just kill them! That's where Margot Anthony and I were so lucky. We had each other to bellyache to and it was a great outlet.

'Wives only congregate in Canberra for the Opening of Parliament and sometimes at Budget time,' said Tam, 'and there's very little organised for them as a group. There's a luncheon traditionally given by the PM's wife at the beginning of the year, but that's about it. So if you do meet another person that you really like you'll probably only see her once a year—the electorate where she lives could be the other side of Australia. That's why I started the Wives' Room in Parliament House.'

Security in Parliament House was a problem and had to be tightened over the years. 'There were various bomb threats which were pretty unpleasant,' said Tam, 'and one day there was a blackout in the House which caused shockwaves amongst the honourable members. But it was only a power failure, nothing sinister.

'But I remember Malcolm coming back to The Lodge one night and saying: "Today was the first time I really thought I'd had it." He'd been standing on the Floor of the House making a speech and suddenly, just in his peripheral vision, he saw an arm swing out in the

Visitors' Gallery and then a white object flying straight towards him through the air.

'So many thoughts can flash through your mind in the space of a second, and he said: "I thought Well, they've got me this time! If I leap under the table it'll probably do no good anyway, and if it's nothing then I'll look a bloody fool. So I just kept talking." And in fact the reports in the papers next day said he didn't pause for an instant—he just kept speaking. The missile was actually an egg thrown by the daughter of a Labor MP.'

Tam's most traumatic experience in Parliament House however was not over a security matter. It was the day Malcolm stood for Leader of the Opposition against Bill Snedden. 'I can still remember sitting in King's Hall waiting for the vote,' she said. 'There was a mob of journalists gathered over in the far corner. They surged down the passage to the party room like water down a plughole when they thought there was a result, and filtered out again when they found no news. I just sat there biting my nails.

'Then in walked a couple of my friends who had been waving *vote Fraser* banners outside Parliament House and they saw I was alone and came and sat with me until the press vortex finally went down for the last time. I saw Alastair Drysdale, Malcolm's press secretary, emerge through the crowd with his hand raised in a V for Victory sign, and so I knew the result before any of the press could tackle me.

'That night I rang Eda from Canberra and said "Quick, Eda! What can I do? I'm about to be interviewed as the wife of the new Leader of the Opposition! How do I make me interesting?" And Eda said, "Tam, you can't, Tam. You'll just have to be yourself and bluff it out!" '

So that's what Tamie did. But often such honesty landed her in trouble.

Chapter 9
BOO-BOOS

'He that can rule his tongue shall live without strife.' Amongst other rather more distinguished places over the years, these words from the book of Ecclesiastes appeared on a sugar sachet in a bowl on the counter of a service station restaurant at Tailem Bend in South Australia, where Tamie happened to call one day for a cup of coffee. The words rang bells in her head and she carried the empty sugar sachet home in her hand-bag to copy them into her scrapbook.

I found them there surrounded by huge exclamation marks and was not surprised. Her recurrent bouts of what we called foot-in-mouth disease were family legend.

'Which particular oral disaster prompted this?' I asked.

'Meekatharra,' she replied, and in an unconscious gesture which amused me even more, put her hand over her mouth.

In October, 1977, the Frasers had flown to Meek-atharra, a small township 800 km north-east of Perth in Western Australia, to attend the annual conference of the Pastoralists and Graziers Association, which Malcolm had been asked to open. At that time the Meekatharra countryside was in its fifth year of drought and there wasn't a blade of grass to be seen—just endless empty desert all around. Some of Malcolm's staff found the scene rather daunting, but Tamie re-velled in it. She loves the wide open spaces and admires

the people with resilience and independence enough
to live there.

The conference in Meekatharra went well and the
Frasers were treated to true outback hospitality. They
flew back to Canberra next day having thoroughly
enjoyed their visit.

'A week or so later I had to address a group of
Greek women at a lunch in Sydney,' said Tam. 'I had
been so impressed by the Meekatharra people, how
their isolation made them dependent on their own
resources, and how this gave them a special calmness
and strength, a sort of quietness behind their faces
which you seldom see in the city. I decided to talk to
the Greek women about isolation in Australia; the
isolation of language and cultural background, and the
isolation of distance. We'd been told that an overseas
jumbo jet had landed at Meekatharra a few weeks
previously, because the Perth airport had been fog-
bound and Meekatharra is Perth's alternate airport.

'I said to my audience: "Can you imagine a group
of migrants from Europe arriving in Australia for the
first time and landing at a place like Meekatharra?
They'd think they had come to the end of the earth!"

'I didn't give the matter another thought until I
happened to be in Perth a week or so later and Lady
Court, the wife of the WA Premier, came up to me
and said: "Tamie dear, don't you think you were a
bit hard on the people of Meekatharra?" I said I loved
Meekatharra, what do you mean? She said, "You said
in Sydney that Meekatharra is the end of the earth.
It was in all the Sunday papers and on the news. And
the people of Meekatharra are so upset, because they'd
really tried to look after you and give you a good
time."'

Tamie was stunned. Immediately she contacted the
Meekatharra district two-way radio service and asked
the manager to explain that it was all a dreadful mis-
understanding. Then she telephoned the people she
had met over there and apologised to them personally,
explaining what had happened and trying to assure
them that she really had enjoyed her visit. But to her

great frustration and regret she felt they remained unconvinced.

A year later the Frasers were attending a Liberal Party conference in Perth when some people from Meekatharra came up to them. 'Tamie, do you remember your visit to Meekatharra?' one of them asked.

'Of course!' said Tamie, with feeling.

'We have a race meeting coming up soon. Why don't you come over and present the Cup?'

'Thank you. I'd like to very much,' she said.

'*What*?!!'

So on October 9, 1978, much to everyone's astonishment, Tamie went back to Meekatharra, fully expecting to be booed out of town. I saw Amanda Derham shortly afterwards and asked her for an account of Meekatharra Revisited.

'Well, it took days and days,' said Amanda, 'by the time we caught planes from Canberra to Melbourne, then Melbourne to Perth, and Perth to Meekatharra—then all the way back again—and it was just before the opening of Parliament, so it was a very busy time. But Mrs. Fraser was determined to go, so off we went.

'We flew over the most amazing country out there! It looked like a moonscape. I've never seen anything like it, so vast and empty, and the further we flew away from Perth the more moonlike it became. There was nothing but flat red desert as far as the eye could see, then suddenly we landed—and there it was! A neat little township with very sensible buildings all carefully laid out in squares—in the middle of endless red dust!

'We had come dressed in our summer whites and after lunch when we arrived at the race course we found the track was two inches deep in dust. The horses raced past and—whoosh, everybody was red! I had dust between my teeth and in my hair and dust under my eyelids, but no-one else seemed to notice, least of all Mrs. Fraser. But I'm city-bred and I found it all rather overwhelming.

'Anyway, everybody seemed to know that Mrs. Fraser had been there before and had called it the end of the earth, and at first you could see them puzzling, wondering why had she come back? Does she really think it's the end of the earth and wants to make sure? Or is it all a bit of a joke? What's she on about? Lots of people had a gentle sort of dig at her, like the pilot of our plane. In a typical laconic Australian drawl, he said: "So you're going back to see if it really is that bad, are you?"

'Actually Mrs. Fraser was quite tense and nervous, but she won everyone over as soon as she arrived,' said Amanda. 'The fact that she had the guts to return won the whole town! At one stage after lunch we were walking down the main street and an enormous man called Tiny—must have been six foot five and at least 20 stone—burst out of the pub nearby and came boring across the street towards us, saying: "G'day, Tamie darlin'! Give 's a great big kiss!" Mrs. Fraser's two security guards who were only half his size went ashen and started to close in, but Tamie turned to him with a beaming smile, and said: "Let's just shake hands for a start!" That diffused the situation beautifully.

'Then on we went to the races and Mrs. Fraser presented The End of the Earth Cup. Everyone was delighted. It all turned out a great success.' Even to the extent, so I heard later on, that on the strength of the occasion some local entrepreneur produced a line of T-shirts bearing the slogan: '*Meekatharra—the end of the earth*" which were worn right across Australia.

Tamie's first public boo-boo—in a long and distinguished line of public boo-boos—occurred only shortly after she was married. Malcolm was scheduled to speak at a naturalisation ceremony for some New Australians at a centre in his electorate, but he had caught a severe cold some days before and completely lost his voice. He asked Tamie to take his place and make the speech for him.

When the day came Tam, with great trepidation, stood up on the dais beside the local Shire President and all the Councillors and at the appropriate moment launched into Malcolm's address. But in her nervousness and haste she failed to notice that Malcolm had (intentionally?) misspelt a vital word, and she found herself proclaiming to her bemused audience that 'We enjoy a high standard of loving in this country!' The comment, coming from a blushing bride just back from her honeymoon, gave great delight to all.

Then there was the furore over Tamie's remarks about the 'dumb electorate'. The night Malcolm was elected Leader of the Opposition in March, 1975, he and Tam appeared on television together. 'The interviewer asked me what sort of leader did I think Malcolm would make,' said Tam, 'and I told him that in my completely neutral, objective and unbiased opinion—smashing! And the interviewer asked why. So I said that I thought Malcolm was very good at explaining things, explaining issues and policies to the dumb electrorate.

'I said I feel I represent the dumb electorate and I went on and on about the bloody dumb electorate. Malcolm was shooting daggers at me from under his eye-brows and the more I tried to back out, the deeper in I went! What I really meant by the remark was that the electorate, being dumb in the sense of not having a voice, needing someone to speak for them. I don't think many people accepted that explanation.'

Neither did I.

Once Malcolm had been elected Prime Minister Tam's penchant for shooting from the lip landed her in even more trouble. Boo-boos in high places are good copy. This fact was brought home to me—and to Tam!—when Chris and I were staying at The Lodge in the winter of 1976. One morning while we were there Tam had to fly off to Sydney to address a women's luncheon. She didn't want to go. 'I've got absolutely nothing to say!' she said, as we were having breakfast together. 'I'm not in a vote-winning *mood*!'

'Never mind, Tam,' said Chris. 'Just tell them some funny stories about one of your trips.'

'I'm not in a *funny* mood, either! In fact, I can't think of a single *amusing remark*!' and off she stormed to the airport.

When she returned that evening we asked her how the speech had gone, and she mumbled: 'Oh, well, you know, I sort of struggled through,' so we thought no more about it.

But next morning *The Australian* carried a banner headline: '*The Random Thoughts of Tamara Fraser*'! under which, complete with irreverent cartoons, were a list of her day's *bon mots*. As Chris pointed out, chuckling into his Weeties, if this were Tam on an off-day, heaven help us all on a good day!

Tamie, shuddering at the memory, has forbidden me to reproduce her comments here, but the most notorious that day was in answer to a question on what drinks were served aboard the royal yacht, *Britannia*: 'Typically British gin and tonic—luke warm and rather flat.'

'I couldn't help it!' she said. 'Someone asked me and the answer just spilled out!' But that remark was to haunt her for years and caused her great embarrassment at Buckingham Palace.

Tamie is short-sighted and wears contact lens, and I remember the story of a policeman pulling her up in her car for speeding, shortly after she acquired them. The policeman asked to see her licence.

'This licence says you should be wearing glasses!' he said.

'Not anymore, Officer,' said Tam. 'I've got contacts.'

'I don't care who you know! You're meant to be wearing glasses!'

For Tamie, contact lens have been a great asset—but occasionally they slip out. She lost one on the Great Wall of China and had half the Australian touring party and their hosts grovelling around in the historic rubble trying to find it. Another one fell into her tropical fruit salad at an official dinner in Port Moresby but that one she managed to retrieve herself, and, causing a minimum of fuss but a few raised eyebrows, dipped it in her mineral water and popped it back.

But on the other hand her contact lens once saved the day. At the beginning of each year Tam used to give a lunch for MPs' wives at The Lodge and this particular year things were a bit sticky. There was some tension at the time with the Country Party over Liberal candidates standing in their electorates, and all the wives were a bit on edge and being ultra-polite. Then, as Tam was serving coffee after the meal, one of her contact lens fell out into a cup. She rushed straight off for a strainer then came back and made a great show of straining the coffee out of all the remaining cups to find it. She soon had everyone laughing and the atmosphere was thawed completely!

When Tam was particularly tired or had been in a smoke-filled room or a dusty atmosphere the contact lens irritated her eyes and made them sore, and so she had to remove them. One night she attended a reception in King's Hall, Parliament House, *sans* her contacts, and towards the end of the evening she looked around for Malcolm.

She saw a figure head and shoulders above the crowd, so she walked up to him, took him by the arm, and said: 'Please take me home, darling. I've had enough.' 'Certainly, darling!', came the astonished reply. It was Gough Whitlam.

But sometimes Tamie's boo-boos weren't really boo-boos at all—just the unlucky result of a cultural gap. In November, 1978, she appeared on television to promote her Australiana Fund and to announce that the four official establishments, including The Lodge, were soon to be opened to the public for the first time. She told her delighted audience that for her there would be no more dashing down the stairs draped in a towel, 'or leaving panties lying in the hall!'

'It was only a line from an old song!' she groaned when she saw the comment featured in the press the next day. 'The song was "The Hostess with the Mostess on the Ball" from the musical "Call Me Madam"!' No-one in the audience had heard of it.

But perhaps Tam's most regretted throw-away line was when she was asked one day did she think Bob Hawke had sex appeal? 'I answered oh well, yes, I suppose so, and shrugged in a non-commital sort of way, and thought no more about it. Next day around

Australia there were banner headlines: "*Tamie Fraser says Bob Hawke is sexy*!" and from then on I was haunted by the remark wherever I went! At every interview or public gathering I attended I was asked, "Did I think Bob Hawke was sexy?" It was a disaster!'

But this time Tamie had the last word. During the 1983 election campaign a zealous reporter asked her yet again if she had said Bob Hawke was sexy. 'Yes, I did say that!' she snapped. 'But let me tell you—it's *policies* not *parts* which win elections!' The reporter looked at her in astonishment, then burst out laughing—and disappeared. And that was the end of the matter.

Tam was forgiven a good deal over the years, I believe, because she never tried to be anything but herself. 'I've always thought the Australian public will give anyone a go—as long as they're fair dinkum,' she told me. 'Whatever you are, they will accept it, but if you try to be what you're not they'll know you're fake. If you try to be posh and you're not posh, they'll know you're fake. If you try to be non-posh and you are posh, they'll know you're fake.

'And I love that thing about the Australian people that they'll give anyone a go—as long as they're genuine; as long as they know who they are themselves.'

Maybe so, but all the same whenever I heard Tamie was off to deliver a speech somewhere I used to ring her up and say: 'Now, Tam, Ecclesiasticus rules— O.K.?' But I'm afraid it never made the slightest bit of difference.

Chapter 10
DRAMA AT CHOGRM

It is a sad reflection on the times that a bomb exploding in a crowded city street, though horrific, is no longer an unprecedented event. Back in 1978, it was.

'I'd never heard a bomb go off before,' said Tam. 'We were fast asleep and suddenly woken by this enormous explosion. It wasn't an ordinary sort of explosion. It was more a reverberation which started somewhere deep inside your stomach and worked its way out. It was quite terrifying. At first, I didn't realise what it was but Malcolm said, "My God! I think that was a bomb!" and then David Burnett burst in to tell us the news.'

This was February, 1978, and the news was that international terrorism had come to Australia. A bomb planted in a rubbish bin outside the front entrance of the Hilton Hotel in Sydney had exploded when it was thrown into a city garbage truck and crushed by the truck's compactor. Two garbage collectors were killed and nine other people injured, one of them critically.

Tamie and Malcolm, along with eleven other heads of state, were staying at the Hilton Hotel that night for the Commonwealth Heads of Government Regional Meeting scheduled to commence at 10 am the next day. Just after midnight David Barnett, Malcolm's press secretary, and Foreign Affairs spokesman David Evans had been in the lobby briefing two reporters when the bomb exploded. They looked at each other in horror, flew down the escalator and out into George Street.

The scene was appalling. There was shattered glass and blood spattered all over the pavement in front of the hotel. Two shockingly mutilated bodies lay on the footpath. A woman in yellow was bending over a third man, a policeman, obviously critically injured. There were fragments of human flesh splattered on the facade of the building and people were screaming and running in all directions. A police car arrived on the scene, siren blaring. David Barnett yelled to the driver to call an ambulance then rushed back inside the hotel and up to the 35th floor to break the news to his PM.

'Malcolm was told not to go down but he threw on his dressing-gown and went straight away,' said Tam. 'He called a meeting with police and security officials in his 8th floor office. They all arrived in their dressing gowns, looking sick with worry. A decision had to be made whether or not to clear the hotel. There were 600 people, including the 12 HOGs and their staff, staying there that night.

'But can you imagine the logistics of evacuating 600 people in the middle of the night? And where would you take them? And how? It was an absolute nightmare! Bomb squad men in blue overalls were sent out with steel prodders to comb the building from the roots of the potted palms to the ducts of the air-conditioning system.

'I was told: "Don't move! Just stay where you are!" and I thought the most helpful thing to do would be to obey. But it wasn't much fun all alone up there, not knowing what the hell was going on. At about 2am Malcolm came back to our room and told me a hessian parcel had just been discovered on the landing of a fire escape and there had been another flurry, but it was only an old brick.

'The tension was unbelievable. Just after two there was a 'phone call warning that another bomb was about to explode, so then the hotel was completely sealed off. No-one was allowed to enter and anyone leaving was not allowed back in. We were prisoners. At about four o'clock Malcolm came back to bed but he had hardly settled for five minutes before there was yet another bomb threat and all of the 7th and 8th floors were cleared. But nothing was found, and by six he was up and dressed again for another security meeting.'

Meanwhile Tam's secretary, Amanda Derham, had been blissfully unaware of the drama, safe in the Land of Nod. 'I slept soundly through the whole thing!' she groaned. 'And when I came down to breakfast all people could talk about was the fact that Andrew Peacock had appeared in silk paisley pyjamas and the PM had a monogram on his pocket!'

As the sun rose to light the scene the whole block between Market and Park Streets looked a complete mess. Hardly a shopfront or a window was left intact and broken glass lay scattered everywhere. There were blood stains on the pavement and an all-pervading smell of garbage from the shell of the wrecked garbage truck nearby. Surprisingly, the waste bin in which the bomb had been planted still sat innocently on the footpath. The day before it had been surrounded by crowds of people who gathered to watch the arrival of the CHOGRM guests and there was even a report that a journalist had confessed rather sheepishly that he had spent at least an hour sitting on it. But although the bin was located within metres of the entrance to the hotel the police admitted they had not foreseen the necessity to search it—testimony to the naivety and inexperience of Australia's security services at that time in dealing with urban terorrism.

The Commonwealth Heads of Government Regional Meeting opened in the ballroom of the Hilton hotel at 10am. 'We all had breakfast in our rooms and then came downstairs for the ceremony.' said Tam.

'Some of the wives were really shaken by the bombing and too nervous to appear—so they stayed in their rooms and didn't come down for a day or two. But most just shrugged it off and got on with the job. And I was so grateful to them for that. I mean, we discussed the bombing, said isn't it frightful, and then we didn't discuss it anymore. It was obviously at the back of our minds, but we didn't let it hang like a thunder cloud above our heads. We went ahead with our program. Adi Lady Lala Mara from Fiji and Mrs. Lee from Singapore were a tremendous support to me in that.'

Meanwhile there was intense speculation in the press as to who had been the target of the bomb. Margaret Jones of *The Sydney Morning Herald* wrote: 'Looking at the Big Twelve lined up behind the nameplates of their countries in the Hilton ballroom, it was difficult not to imagine a question mark hanging over the head of each. Was the bomber a lone eccentric with a general hatred of politicians and other great ones, or was there a specific target for his protest?

'The guessing game went on all day. Was it Tonga, Nauru, Western Samoa or Fiji? Surely not. Mr. Michael Somare of PNG has his enemies, but seems high on the list of improbables. The abortion lobby has reason to dislike Mr. Muldoon (of New Zealand), but would they blow him up?

'Mr. Lee Kuan Yew, Datuk Onn of Malaysia, Mr. Jayawardene of Sri Lanka and General Ziaur Rahmen of Bangladesh all have troubles at home. Each could be a target. So could, if it comes to that, Malcolm Fraser . . .

'At least one of the possible targets remains quite unmoved. At 82, Mr. Morarji Desai (of India) appears calm, quite ageless, and likely to see out the end of the century at least. He heard the blast in his Hilton suite, but having remarked it, went back to sleep. "One is not fearful of these sorts of happenings," he says. "If one is afraid, life is not worthwhile."' As investigations were later to reveal, Mr. Desai had no reason for such equanimity. It is generally accepted that he was the target of the bomb.

After the Opening ceremony Commonwealth Secretary General Mr. Shridath Ramphal gave a luncheon at the Hilton for the Heads of Delegations to meet the press, while Tamie and Margot Anthony took the wives off to lunch at Old Government House, Parramatta. They were a diverse group, some in western dress, others in their national costumes. From Fiji there was Adi, Lady Lala Mara, whose interests included the welfare of women and children and reviving traditional arts and crafts. Then there was Mrs. Lee, wife of Lee Kuan Yew, an MA and a barrister, educated at Raffles College before reading law at Cambridge University; Mrs. Padma Desai, the Indian PM's daughter-in-law who enjoyed reading, gardening and knitting; Mrs. Elina Jayawardene from Sri Lanka and from Malaysia Datin Suhailah Hussein, who listed her interests as Girl Guides, child welfare and education, gardening, glass-cutting, flower-arranging, and antiques. As well there was Mrs. Thea Muldoon from New Zealand who pursued horticulture, Ikebana and the welfare of women and children, and Madame Christina Dowiyogo from Nauru who said her interests centred on the home.

'We took them all to Old Government House, Parramatta, so they could see one of the finest collections of Australian furniture on public view,' said Tam. 'Dame Helen Blaxland was there to greet them and show them around. The collection has been beautifully put together by the National Trust women in NSW and the CHOGRM wives were genuinely interested to see it. And you can tell if people aren't interested— they get a kind of glaze—but these women really were, and as a result when we went to Bowral next day they asked to visit some antique shops to see if any similar furniture was available.'

In the afternoon Tamie had planned to take the visitors to a Koala Park in West Pennant Hills, but the police said they were unable to guarantee its security so the visit had to be cancelled. So Tam slipped away with Malcolm to the Sydney hospital to visit the people who had been injured in the bombing. 'I felt sorry for them being confronted by us and our menagerie!' she said. 'There was always a menagerie travelling with us wherever we went, security and staff etc. and I kept thinking those poor men lying there feeling absolutely bloody and how the very last thing they'd want to see was the Prime Minister and his wife smiling down at them with fangs bared, however sincerely.

'And yet Malcolm and I felt we must tell them how sorry we were, say to them we are desperately sorry we have done this to you. We really did so want them to know how upset we were for them and their families, the ones who may be badly injured for the rest of their lives. How do you convey this, and not let them think you're only there as a PR exercise? I only hope they understood . . .'

The next day while Singapore's Lee Kuan Yew was calling on his fellow heads of government at the meeting for 'an act of political will' to foster closer economic co-operation and expand trade between the 12 Asian and Pacific Commonwealth nations, Mrs. Leo Port, the wife of the Lord Mayor, gave a lunch for the visiting wives at Sydney's Town Hall.

'It hadn't really been brought home to me until then how serious the security problem was,' Amanda Derham told me. 'I had been so busy worrying about the details of my job—things like whether the cars would arrive or not, and should the photographers be shuffled out now, where should we be in five minutes and how on earth can I get those two to stop talking—that I really hadn't been aware of the tension and the danger. But I'll never forget standing with Mrs. Desai (Mr. Desai's daughter-in-law) by the entrance to the town hall after lunch that day, waiting for her car to arrive.

'We stood there waiting by the entrance and a security man came up and grabbed her and took her right back inside, and said: "Madam, please wait back here!" And I'd been naively saying the car will be here in a moment, shall we stand outside in the sunshine? Then when the car did come she was literally picked up by the elbows by two huge security guards and shoved into the back seat. And you could see the look of relief on their faces when she drove away.'

Most Commonwealth Heads of Government meetings have a retreat, a place where the heads of state can go without staff to relax for a few days of informal discussion. What Gleneagles in Scotland was to CHOGM, Berrida Manor at Bowral was to CHOGRM.

'Originally we were scheduled to travel to Bowral by train late that afternoon,' said Tam, 'but after the bombing that was not considered safe so the police decided to use army helicopters instead. Everything was kept a total secret—what time we were leaving and from where—and even our driver as we left the hotel wasn't sure exactly where to take us, which oval out at Moore Park. But as we approached we could see two helicopters waiting and we drove up to them and climbed in—Andrew Peacock took one lot of guests and we the other. Doug and Margot Anthony were with us too.

'They weren't luxurious VIP helicopters either, just standard army Chinooks, very sparse. We sat strapped in tightly together down each side and secured to the floor in front of us was special emergency medical equipment—stretchers, bottles of plasma, a cylinder of oxygen, the works—and we had to sit and stare at it the whole journey!

'A soldier with a gun across his shoulders stood in the open doorway of the helicopter with his hands behind his back, and as we took off it was all I could do to stop myself leaning forward and grabbing on to his belt to stop him toppling out. And he rode the whole way to Bowral standing with his back to that open door!'

Meanwhile back at Central railway station red carpets had been laid out on the No. 1 Platform but six minutes before departure time they were rolled up again. Food and drink had been loaded on to the train but just before departure time two trolleys were wheeled up and the food and drink taken out. At 5.45 pm and 30 seconds late the train which was to have taken the HOG's 130 k's to Bowral pulled out from the station—empty. It ran only as far as Flemington, and stopped. By then its intended cargo was safely in the air. The Bowral station had been repainted for nothing.

Once the party had landed safely on a golf course at Bowral and walked through the lovely grounds to Berrida Manor, the tension eased considerably. Berrida Manor is a motel/health resort developed around a picturesque old two-storey red brick homestead covered with creepers. It has a beautiful garden, tennis courts, a gym and a spa, and comfortable, attractive accommodation. 'It was just perfect for the purpose,' said Amanda, 'but Mrs. Fraser and I had dreadful trouble placing the visitors in appropriate rooms! Because, as Mrs. Fraser pointed out, not everybody sleeps with their husband. And who does and who doesn't? And do you ask or don't you? Anyway, it was decided we wouldn't ask, and we would assume they didn't, and so provide a sort of suite—two rooms and a small sitting room—and they could do what they liked! It all seemed to work out in the end!'

Security still loomed large. 'They imported potted plants,' said Amanda, 'and there were potted plants everywhere with big burly policemen trying to hide behind them. The first morning I got up early and saw Mr. and Mrs. Lee come in dressed in their walking gear—they'd obviously been out for an early morning constitutional—and there were security men standing around behind trees all over the place trying to be unobtrusive! It was all a bit bizarre.'

For Tamie it was all a bit bizarre that evening when her official dinner took four hours to be served. 'Dinner that night at Berrida Manor was the first really relaxed affair of the visit,' said Tam. 'Here we were safe at last in the peaceful countryside, and birds were singing and it was a beautiful evening.

'We sat down for dinner and the tables looked pretty and welcoming and the first course was served—a choice of asparagus or scallops in a light mushroom sauce I think it was, and that was delicious, but then the second course didn't come and we waited and waited.

'Apparently our hostess was watching the "Duchess

of Duke Street" on the TV and had forgotten to put on the vegetables and it took four hours for 20 people to be served! It was just desperate! We were sitting at tables of four or six or and it's all very well, I mean, of course you enjoy peoples' company, but for *four hours*? It was bad news! I'll never forget it!

'But the evening was saved by the New England Ensemble. They were a group who'd had an enormously successful overseas concert tour. Playing background music wasn't their thing at all and they were doing us a tremendous favour to be there. They played most beautifully, and as the evening dragged on and on they just kept playing. They were grey with weakness, dropping with exhaustion by the end of it but they played on and on and they saved the night! They were quite wonderful!'

The next night the visitors were taken to dinner at Retford Park, Mr. James Fairfax's home nearby. 'It's a lovely place to take visitors and we were so grateful to James Fairfax for having us,' said Tam. 'He showed us his collection of Australian paintings and sculpture then led us into the diningroom for dinner. Around the wall he has a wonderful mural by Donald Friend and the room looked so charming and warm and inviting.

'We were shown to our places and as I sat down I was hit by an overwhelming smell of garlic, an unbelievable smell of garlic! My eyes started to weep and I was gasping with the fumes and I thought, "James has gone mad! What on earth has he chosen for a first course?" But it was a special meal for Mr. Desai who was sitting next to me. He was a strict vegetarian and he had four tablespoons of crushed garlic, raw, waiting for him on his plate!'

Next day the visitors travelled back to Sydney by car and again maximum security was enforced. 'There was a tank stationed every few miles along the road and at each cross-road,' said Tam. 'They were positioned as discreetly as possible, behind a tree or something, but they were still visible, and soldiers with machine guns were guarding every bridge and overpass. It's not the sort of sight we're used to here, thank heaven, and it seemed so terribly un-Australian. But the Army responded in a brilliant way. This was a real emergency, and with only a day's notice they handled the operation with true military precision. It was very comforting.'

'Is this gathering just an expensive waste of time?', Malcolm Booker had asked in the *Canberra Times* at the beginning of the conference. At its close on Thursday, February 16, Singapore's Lee Kuan Yew, unusual among Asian politicians for his public bluntness, told a Press conference: 'I am leaving agreeably surprised.'

The meeting issued a 15-page 45-point communique listing some useful joint initiatives: groups to promote trade within the region, joint action on drugs and terrorism, and energy research. But the main topic was trade and tariffs and the communique called on the industrialised countries to improve access for manufactures from the developing nations, and Australia's record in this area was only criticised by general implication which was regarded as a great concession.

All the leaders said the talks had been worthwhile and agreed to meet again in two years time. As this had been the first Pacific area regional conference and Malcolm's own personal initiative taken at Gleneagles the year before, he was well pleased. But the bombing at the Hilton overshadowed everything and it was with some relief that Tamie and Malcolm farewelled the HOGs on the last day and flew back for a few days rest at Nareen.

Later Malcolm told us: 'One thing about the bomb incident in Sydney: you suggest the target was probably Mr. Desai, and that's right. It was almost certainly Ananda Marga, but that was never proved. But there were two entrances to the Hilton, and I believe both he and I owe our lives to Mr. Muldoon!

'There was a group of pro-abortion women outside the hotel to give Mr. Muldoon a noisy, hostile welcome. I thought we couldn't have Mr. Muldoon as the only person with a hostile welcome, so we should switch the welcome for him to the other side of the hotel.

'Muldoon was coming about 4.30pm and Desai about 5pm, so we switched the meeting to the opposite side of the hotel for Muldoon, we also greeted Desai on the same side as Muldoon, that was the other side of the hotel from the explosion.

'If it was a radio-controlled bomb and intended to blow it up when Desai was being greeted, there would have been 50 or 60 people killed.'

Chapter 11
NAREEN

Nareen is safety and sanctuary, refuge and retreat. Nareen, in a word, is home.

Situated about 30 km from Coleraine in far western Victoria in the heart of Malcolm's Wannon electorate, Nareen is the sheep and cattle property owned by the Fraser family since 1945. During the years that Malcolm was PM, Tamie spent all the school holidays there with the children, and as many stolen days or weekends as possible in between. Malcolm came as often as he could. It was a place of healing and restoration for them both.

The homestead at Nareen was built in 1890 and took five years to construct. It has a verandah running along its entire length on both sides, trimmed with lattice arches. Inside, the rooms are set each side of a long central passage. The garden is extensive, full of lovely old trees and sweeping lawns interspersed with bright banks of flowers carefully chosen for an aesthetic balance of density, colour and size.

In the northern section of the garden, just inside the hedge, there is a grove of camellias, Malcolm's pride and joy. All the family have camellias in their gardens which Malcolm grew from cuttings.

In a narrow bed along the front verandah stands a row of hydrangeas which has been there as long as I can remember—and has caused trouble as long as I can remember.

One of the gardening jobs Malcolm used to under-

take with particular relish was pruning, and with se-
cateurs in hand he was utterly ruthless. In half an hour
he would reduce a row of flourishing hydrangea bushes
to a few bare sticks in the ground. The fact that they
were invariably magnificent again the following year
reduced Tamie's anguish not at all. 'Why can't you
stick to pruning the bureaucracy instead of pruning
the garden?' I heard her sigh one day in despair, to
which he mumbled in reply that in the garden it was
so much easier to get rid of all the bloody dead wood.

Wannon was a Labor-held seat until 1955 when
Malcolm, with the aid of DLP preferences, captured
it for the Liberal Party. From then on he set out to
make it his own. He visited every tiny branch or centre
in the electorate as often as possible, advertising in the
local press the time and place at which he would be
available so that people could come and see him and
discuss their problems. These Grumble Sessions, as
he called them, were an invaluable way of keeping in
touch with the needs and opinions of his electorate.

He attended endless Liberal Party branch meetings
too, often travelling long distances at night to address
only a few loyal supporters. I remember one time in
the very early days my mother and father going along
to a Liberal Party meeting in Caramut, a small town
near Nareeb Nareeb, to hear Malcolm speak. Mum
had been saying how much she was looking forward
to it, how seldom she had a chance to hear her son-
in-law on the rostrum and generally making a Big Deal
of the event. On the appointed night she and Dad
arrived at the Caramut hall in plenty of time to obtain
a good seat.

Malcolm arrived with Tamie shortly afterwards.
They all sat together in the car outside the hall, waiting.
And waiting. And waiting. Not another soul appeared. As they were about to leave a battered old
utility roared up and out jumped the local branch
president, covered in grass seeds. 'Sorry no-one's
turned up!' he said. 'We're all out hay-making! Would
you mind coming back another night?'

Another night in another town Malcolm delivered

an address to an audience of one. It was again at a tiny centre miles from anywhere and when only a single person turned up to listen to him Malcolm said, half-jokingly: 'You don't want to hear my speech all on your own, do you?'

'If I don't know your policies, how can I vote for you?' the man replied. So Malcolm mounted the steps of the stage without further comment and began his speech while his lone audience sat at the back of the hall in silence. After about five minutes, Malcolm said: 'Will that do?'

'If that's all the policy you're got, you're not worth voting for,' said the man. So Malcolm continued his address on the state of the nation and the problems of the world for another 20 minutes, until his audience finally called out: 'Okay, that'll do. Let's go down to the pub!'

Knowing Malcolm I find the story entirely believable. On occasion, over the years, he has been compared with Sir Robert Menzies in some aspects of his philosophy and approach but as Tamie once pointed out, in this facet of their characters they were opposites. On the platform Sir Robert used to be highly impatient with people who asked stupid questions. He put them down mercilessly. 'Whereas Malcolm is the other way,' said Tam. 'He drives everyone mad by explaining on and on and on to a little old lady what he's already said on and on and on in his primary speech!'

Over the years Malcolm built up a reputation in his electorate for being an always accessible local member. I remember Dad coming home from Hamilton one day with his eyes dancing because someone had stopped him in the street and said how wonderful it was the way Malcolm exposed himself so readily to the public. For a family like ours of course the comment was a gift and for years afterwards Malcolm could never leave for a political function without someone saying: 'Off to expose yourself to the public again, eh, Mal?' 'But the problem with being always so accessible,' said Tam, 'was that when Malcolm was made a Minister in 1966, everyone resented the time he had to spend away from the electorate. People still expected him to be at their beck and call, and the fact that as a Minister he now had the whole of Australia for his electorate didn't seem to make any difference. But interestingly, once he became Prime Minister people understood totally that he wouldn't have time to do as much as he'd previously done in the electorate, and they were understanding about it.'

But a Prime Minister still has the duties and responsibilities of a local member and the Frasers continued to do as much as possible in the electorate. Their diaries tell the story: Opened new wing Portland and District Hospital; handed over remedial teaching bus to Casterton school; attended art and craft exhibition, Hamilton Art Gallery; unveiled centennary plaque, Harrow school; opened new social rooms, Coleraine Football Club; guest speaker Red Cross lunch, Hamilton; opened surf carnival, Warrnambool—the list goes on and on, sometimes there must have been moments when they wondered if it were all worthwhile.

For instance, on one occasion when Tamie was terribly tired and busy and only at Nareen for one day, she spent the entire afternoon driving to the outer reaches of the electorate to visit an Old People's Home.

'I was taken around the home to meet all these old darlings in wheel chairs,' said Tam, 'and as we approached one old dear the nurse in charge said to her: "Look Mrs. Whatnot, here's the wife of the Prime Minister to meet you!" and the old lady's face lit up with a smile of such warmth and appreciation. "Why, hello, Mrs. Menzies!" she said.'

During any spare hours at Nareen Tam loved to work in the garden while Malcolm rode around the paddocks on his motorbike checking the cattle, or fished for rainbow trout in the big fresh-water dam just beyond the homestead.

My father was responsible for Malcolm's love of fishing. It started a long time ago when a severe bout of hepatitis forced Malcolm to take three months complete rest. Such idleness was anathema to him.

He was like a caged lion and nearly drove the family mad, so Dad took him in hand and they spent hours together with fishing rods in hand while Malcolm was given instructions on how to cast a fly at a large white dinner plate placed strategically in the middle of the front lawn. Fishing proved a perfect antidote to the pressures of political life, but Tamie used to tease Dad that it was all his fault that every single holiday she had ever had since, was a fishing holiday.

Over the years all the children became keen on fishing as well, so Tam, finally accepting the wisdom of the premise If You Can't Lick 'em, Join 'em, learnt to cast a pretty mean fly herself and Dad's piscatorial victory was absolute one day when he was ill in bed at Nareeb Nareeb, and in Tamie walked to present to him for his dinner a 2 lb trout she had caught that morning in the dam at Nareen.

Over the years the Frasers entertained many overseas visitors at Nareen. Usually they had a picnic in the paddocks, dinner at night with some of their local friends, and probably some fishing, a game of tennis or clay-bird shooting next day. I remember Lee Kuan Yew and Mrs. Lee coming to stay at Nareen to see the total eclipse of the sun. The issue of Aboriginal land rights was dominating politics in Canberra at the time and a bus load of Aborigines came up to demonstrate outside the front gate.

The morning Mr. and Mrs. Lee were due to arrive the station overseer came to the homestead, and said: 'Mrs. Fraser, what'll I do? There's some black thunder clouds rumbling down at the front gate.' Tamie glanced out the window, said: 'But there's not a cloud in the sky!' which gave us all great enjoyment at her expense. The drive at Nareen is a mile long but we could still hear the noise of the demonstrators clearly from the homestead and their screaming and chanting continued well into the night.

Canadians John Turner and his wife Geills were guests at Nareen whenever they came to Australia, which was quite frequently after John had resigned from Pierre Trudeau's cabinet. An old Oxford friend of Malcolm's and a most charming man, John Turner was claiming at the time to dinner guests like us how good it was to be out of politics and free from any further political ambition. I don't know what he was saying to Malcolm in private. He is currently Leader of the Canadian Opposition.

Princess Alexandra and the Hon. Angus Ogilvy came to Nareen for a few days one spring. Just before they arrived Tam rang me and said: 'Help, Pete! I want to take the Princess on a picnic in the Black Range. I need a suitable spot—somewhere which has Scenes of Unparalleled Grandeur, a Tinkling Stream and abundant F & F (flora and fauna). Could you do a recci for me?'

So a friend and I drove around the rough bush tracks through the mountains north east of Balmoral sussing out a venue for the right royal picnic. But when we found a scene of unparalleled grandeur it had very little flora and fauna, and when we found flora and fauna there was no tinkling stream, and when at last we found a stream it was tinkling through a caravan park. Eventually, about sundown we came across a little secluded gully full of wild flowers, and reported our find to Tam.

However, when the big day came, the royal visitors said why travel all that way when there couldn't be a lovelier spot for a picnic than in the paddocks at Nareen?

Why indeed? No ordinary home in country Australia is wired up to the extent that every passing butterfly sounds sirens in three states and a roving possum can bring out the bomb squad. But then Nareen at that time was no ordinary home. Security measures were undertaken slowly and reluctantly, but they were a necessity.

'At first, I was allowed to be expendable!' said Tam. 'Security officers were only stationed at Nareen when Malcolm was home. Then one night when I was here on my own, sitting reading in front of the fire, I heard a knock at the front door (it was about 10 pm) and when I opened it, there was a strange man standing on the doorstep.

'He said to me very politely: "May I come in?" and he came in, and then he said: "How do you do, Mrs. Fraser? I'm God." "Oh," I replied. "How nice to meet you, God!" "Yes," he said, "I'm God, and I've come all the way from Lismore to see you." So we had a long chat, and in the end I said, "Thank you, God, for visiting me and I will pray to you each night, but now would you *kindly leave*?" And he did, and it was all very good-natured and amicable, but when the security staff heard about it they nearly had a fit and more precautions had to be installed.'

In the early days a rostered security officer was on duty in the homestead whenever the Frasers were there, but later on the security staff were set up independently in a vacant station hand's cottage by the main gate. A proper sentry box was erected for the guards and all callers were carefully checked in and out. It was then felt that no-one could come or go without security's knowledge or consent.

But not so. I remember well one night when Christopher and I were going to the same dinner party as Tam and, knowing she was on her own, had arranged to call in at Nareen to give her a lift. When the night arrived our baby was ill so I was unable to go, but Christopher set off as planned, collected Tamie from Nareen, and drove on with her to the party.

At about ten-thirty my telephone rang. It was Malcolm, calling from Canberra. 'Pete, I've lost Tamie!' he thundered, his voice a mixture of anxiety and rage. 'Do you know where the hell she might be?'

'Yes, Mal,' I answered calmly. 'Chris has taken her to dinner at the Richardsons.'

'Well, thank God for that! Security at Nareen swears she's at the homestead, but I've been ringing all evening and can't get an answer.'

'Course not,' I said. 'Tam's playing bridge at Willaroo and probably half-way through her second rubber by now. So if you want to speak to her there, here's the number,' and I smiled to myself as I reeled it off, knowing full well he would.

Malcolm was always ringing Tamie on the telephone. There was never a weekend, a night or merely a lunch that Tamie was not called away at some stage to speak to Our Pal Mal, as we call him. From all over Australia, indeed, from all over the world, he would ring her any hour of the night or day.

In most households a telephone ringing in the dead of night brings instant dread. But with Tamie in the house we knew immediately there was no need to worry, and we'd just turn over and go back to sleep, leaving her to it. Commentators often wrote that for Malcolm the telephone was a weapon. We knew it was also a lifeline.

But the security guards at Nareen were mostly highly efficient and unobtrusive. I remember Hugh Fraser telling me about his big brother Mark one night taking a gun and going out into the garden to shoot a rabbit which had been living in the park area beyond the tennis court and eating all the young trees. Just after dusk he crept out, moving soundlessly from cover to cover amongst the trees he knew so well since childhood.

When he reached the park he saw the rabbit grazing. He raised his gun and shot it clean. A split second later he heard an unmistakable *click*! close by. He froze and cried out his name!

From out of the bushes behind him emerged a security officer, lowering his pump-action shotgun from his shoulder. 'Listen young fella,' said the security officer, white-faced and shaking. 'Please, never, *never* do that again!' Mark mumbled his apologies, and went his way.

'Then there was the incident of the threatening note in 1975,' said Tamie. 'Malcolm was still leader of the Opposition and it was during all the drama over Supply and things were red hot. And we received this nasty threat that the police were taking very seriously that someone was going to come and maim the family—maim, rather than kill anyone, but still pretty horrible.

'The children were at home for the weekend with friends from school and we had a Garden Party here on the Sunday in aid of the National Trust, so I thought, as it was going to be dangerous at home, I'd send them out into the paddocks for a picnic—cook some chops, etc., and I'd come out and join them later when I could get away.

'Security had the homestead all sealed off but the garden was full of people, and Malcolm and I planned to join the party during the afternoon. But before lunch he was on the phone and I was wanting to take the kids' picnic out to them in the paddocks. So in the end I got sick of waiting and scribbled a note on a piece of paper with a black texta and held it up under his nose to show him, then off I went.

'When I arrived back again I found an atmosphere of near seige! All the security officers were rushing round in circles, and every telephone occupied! "What the hell's going on?" I demanded. "Oh, nothing, Mrs. Fraser, nothing at all!" said the chief security man. "Listen, you must *tell* me!" I said. "Even if it's really bad, I would rather know!" "Well, as a matter of fact we do have a slight problem," he said. "We found this threatening note on the table by the telephone. Take a look at it." And there in letters of big black texta was my note to Malcolm: "*I'll fix the kids and be back after lunch for you!*"'

Chapter 12
HER LOWEST HOUR

Parliamentary privilege is a two-edged sword. Essential in a democracy for the fearless exposure of corruption or the abuse of power, it can also, under its immunity from the laws of libel, defame innocent people. I know, because in 1979 it happened to my family. But the real target, of course, was the Prime Minister.

In the aftermath of the bushfires of 1977 the Victorian government had made loans available at concessional rates, through the Rural Finance Commission, to farmers who had suffered heavy losses. My brother Hugh Beggs applied for one of these loans. 'I went along to the Rural Finance Commission like every other farmer who had been burnt out,' Hugh said, 'explained to them the extent of my problem and asked for finance to cover it.

'The amounts were quite large because our losses were quite large—50 miles of fencing at roughly $3500 per mile for a start, plus 3000 stud sheep, although stud sheep are really irreplaceable. Anyway, I applied for two loans—one at the concessional interest rate and the other at a normal commercial rate. I told the head of Rural Finance that the Prime Minister's wife was my sister, and asked that he make sure that, within the guidelines laid down, this transaction be absolutely proper and correct.'

The application was processed and approved in the usual way and Hugh turned his attention to the enormous task of rebuilding his enterprise.

About twelve months later Hugh told me he was attending a Victorian Farmers and Graziers Meeting at Farrer House in Melbourne when he received a phone call from the head of the Rural Finance Commission informing him that someone had been probing into his affairs.

He left the meeting immediately, went straight around to the Commission and, with the head, again checked through the loan transactions with a fine tooth comb. 'Finding everything in perfect order as expected I just thought, "What bastards!", then went home and forgot about it,' he said.

Roughly a year later, in March 1979, none of us could believe our ears when Mr. Brian Howe, a Victorian Labor MP, in an attempt to impugn the integrity of the Prime Minister, raised the matter of the Beggs family loan in Federal parliament, questioning its propriety. Next day the matter was blazing headlines around the country.

Tamie was aghast. 'I was in Sydney,' she said. 'I was going to an art exhibition at the Opera House. A reporter stopped me on the pavement as soon as I got out of the car. David Barnett, Malcolm's press secretary, had told me not to comment, but I was so white with rage, I was so speechless with anger—that my family should have been innocently dragged into the political mire because of me.

'I don't know what questions that reporter asked. I didn't care what questions he asked. I was going to tell him exactly what I thought of it before he even opened his mouth!'

'And she really meant it,' said Amanda Derham, who was in Sydney with Tam that day. 'She fairly flew at him! She was spitting out her words! And in the end she said: "I think anyone who attacks a retired man under parliamentary privilege is *lower than a snake's duodenum!*" Then she took a deep breath and gathered herself together, as she was very able to do, put her handbag under her arm, and walked off with great dignity.'

The comment made headlines. It also made the point.

'We went straight on into the exhibition,' Amanda continued, 'and immediately Mrs. Fraser had to bury it all and turn into the charming and consummate guest speaker which everyone was expecting. She did it magnificently, but she was still shaking so much that when someone handed her a glass of champagne she spilt most of it on the floor.'

The family's initial response to the furore was: no comment. These were private affairs and we would not discuss them in public. But other people were speaking out in our defence. Mr. Rupert Hamer, the then Premier of Victoria, told the press that claims about the loans to the family of the Prime Minister's wife were utterly despicable. He said Mr. Howe's allegations 'were factually wrong and a scurrilous attack.' The Victorian Minister for Lands, Mr. Borthwick, said: 'If ever a family could have been said to be in a position to use political clout, they were, but they did not do so.'

But the clamour continued and the family felt thoroughly under seige in the face of Howe's attack. I can't begin to describe how helpless and frustrated you feel in that kind of situation, knowing you are innocent but wondering whether people believe you— wondering whether they are looking at you sideways and thinking where there's smoke, &c. &c. We stuck it out in silence for about two days while the media speculated, the politicians attacked and my father absolutely squirmed in his seat.

He simply could not understand, after the way he had lived his life, how anyone could consider that sort of thing against him. 'I was squirming too,' said Hugh, 'because it was me who should have borne the brunt of the attack. It was me and not Dad who arranged the loans. Dad never went near the Rural Finance Commission in his life.'

Then slowly the tone of reporting began to change. 'We have telephoned every farmer in the telephone book who lives near Nareeb Nareeb,' said a reporter on the television news one night, 'and all of them, to a man, were vehement in their defence of Sandford Beggs. Now you'd think after living all your life in the one place there'd be *someone* who had a grudge against you. We could find no-one who didn't hold him in the highest regard.'

Early the next morning Hugh received a call from a journalist representing a major TV current affairs program. He told Hugh he had investigated the Beggs family affairs in depth and had found absolutely nothing untoward. 'He said he thought we'd been given a raw deal,' said Hugh, 'and asked would I like an opportunity to put our side of the argument on television? I said perhaps that would be a good idea, but first I wanted to confer with the family.' The family agreed things had gone far enough. Hugh was asked, on our behalf, to put the record straight.

Two hours later a helicopter landed in the front paddock of Nareeb Nareeb, scattering dust, dry grass and stray cockatoos in all directions. 'The journalist sat me on a log and I told him the facts,' said Hugh. He told them simply but with force. They were unanswerable.

Back in Canberra the Prime Minister had been struggling in his attempts to contain the affair politically. He tabled countless documents, but politics is not always about facts and the matter had continued to boil. Ironically, what really diffused the issue in the end was Tam's throw-away remark about the snake's duodenum. I admit to a certain grim satisfaction upon hearing that, for a long time afterwards, Brian Howe could not rise to his feet in the House without being greeted by a cry of *hissssssssssssssssss*.

Hugh, reflecting on the episode a long time afterwards, said he felt it was a case of a character assassination attempt—which had failed. 'At least I like to think it failed,' he said. 'The media's priorities are rather strange. The Beggs' loan kept China's invasion of Vietnam off the front pages for three days, but journalists like Mike Willesee and *The Age* "Insight" team made their own investigations and finding no wrong gave me a chance to answer, then dropped the issue, and that was the end of it. That gave me some faith in the freedom and responsibility of the press. But the trouble is, of course, that the written word is like a stone thrown—you can never bring it back, and I don't think the scars ever healed in Dad.'

Nor in Tam. For her, I think, this episode was the worst she ever experienced in all the years she was the wife of the PM. Worse than any of the resignations which plagued Malcolm's Ministry, worse than any of the violence to which she and Malcolm were subjected, worse than any barrages from the press or political storms—this dragging of her family's private affairs through the public arena, I believe, was her lowest hour.

At the height of the clamour I received in the mail a letter from Tam, which, in startlingly uncharacteristic terms, laid her anguish bare. The letter contained no news nor salutation, just these words from Oscar Wilde:

> . . . Nature, whose sweet rains fall on unjust and just alike, will have clefts in the rocks where I may hide, and secret valleys where I may weep undisturbed. She will hang the night with stars so that I may walk abroad in the darkness without stumbling and send the wind over my foot prints, so that none may track me to my hurt . . .

I sent back to her by return mail, from Gibran:

> 'But you, child of space, you restless in rest, you shall not be trapped nor tamed . . .
>
> You shall not fold your wings that you may pass through doors, nor bend your head that it strikes not against a ceiling, nor fear to breathe less walls should crack and fall down . . .
>
> For that which is boundless in you abides in the mansion of the sky, whose door is the morning mist, and whose windows are the songs and silences of the night.

Neither of us ever mentioned the exchange again.

Chapter 13
NIGERIA—ZAMBIA

When you have a sister overseas on Official Tour at least you know she must have arrived safely at each destination because if she hasn't, it will be front page news. With the Frasers away travelling, many's the morning I turned on the radio first thing and lay in bed listening intently until the headlines were over. On the other hand, Grannie and Grandfather's chief dread when they were In Charge, was that if something did happen they would never be able to reach the Fraser children in time before the children heard the news on the radio or watched it in living colour on TV.

'There was only one time when I thought we really mightn't get back,' said Tam one day when I raised the subject. 'It was in July/August 1979 when we went to Nigeria and Zambia for the Commonwealth Heads of Government Conference. There'd been a lot of violence leading up to it, a lot of unrest in Africa over Rhodesia's independence.

'Bishop Muzorewa was in charge in Rhodesia and wasn't liked by either side, and the whole continent was really trembling. An aeroplane was shot down over the Zambian border just before we left because it was in the wrong airspace, and we had to fly hundreds of miles out of our way to be certain of staying in safe air corridors. It was just a year after the Hilton bombing at CHOGM in Sydney, and altogether I really believed before we went that we may not return.'

So Tam wrote a special letter to each of the children and hid the letters in her jumper drawer. 'When we got back from Africa I didn't read them again, I just tore them up and put them in the wastepaper basket and thought what a stupid woman.'

Malcolm had been invited to hold some informal pre-CHOGM talks in Lagos with General Obasanjo, Head of the Nigerian Military Government, about the situation in Rhodesia. 'Nigeria was very important in terms of a Zimbabwe settlement,' Malcolm told me, 'and as General Obasanjo was not attending the Lusaka conference it seemed a good idea to meet him first and hear his views.'

The two men had useful discussions facilitated by an immediate sense of mutual respect, which was to develop into a close working partnership seven years later when they served together as co-chairmen of the Commonwealth Eminent Persons Group on Southern Africa. 'General Olusegun Obasanjo is a most unusual man,' Malcolm said recently. 'He was in the army in Nigeria and over the years there'd been a number of coups, mostly military coups, and a number of ex-Presidents had been killed in the process.

'General Obasanjo took over one coup that was going wrong and became head of a Military Government there in 1976. But he believed that government was not a job for generals, and over the next three years set up a democracy in Nigeria. He drew up a constitution allowing for three tiers of government—local, state and federal, and then held local elections, then state elections, and finally federal elections—and at none of these elections did he stand himself. And when a civilian government was in place he even decided he couldn't stay in the Army because the new government would always be wondering when he was going to lead another coup. So he resigned and became a farmer. I think he now runs about 600,000 layer hens. He's a very great man.'

Tam was reluctant to say much about her visit to Africa in 1979. With the political situation there so finely balanced and Malcolm playing a continuing and influential role she was unusually circumspect in what she revealed about the trip, and I finally heard an account of it from Amanda Derham over lunch one day in Melbourne.

'There were about twenty people plus press in the Australian touring party,' Amanda told me, 'and when we landed at Lagos airport amidst tight security there was a brass band to greet us and a guard of honour and General Obasanjo was there, plus lots of other Nigerian officials looking wonderfully colourful in their flowing national dress. But all around the perimeter of the airport there were soldiers in battle-dress, guns at the ready. Soldiers with guns is not the kind of greeting you're used to in Australia.

'After the welcoming ceremony the Australians were taken to the official Nigerian guest house in Lagos, a closed-in concrete building on a beach, over-looking a large expanse of black sand. On the foreshore there were lots of people parading up and down; tall, magnificent-looking black women wearing their traditional costumes of blues and reds with lots of white.'

The next morning, after laying a wreath on the Cenotaph in Tafawa Bulewa Square, the Frasers and some of their party were driven to Ibadan in Oyo State, about 150k's from Lagos. 'Ibadan had open drains and children were playing in the piles of rubbish which littered the streets,' Amanda told me. 'The PM had come to visit the Olubadan, Obe Akinbiyi, who lived there. The Olubadan was a tribal chief or prince. He lived in a big two-storied house which stood out from all the other houses in the street. When we went inside it almost felt like being in a temple.

'There in the dim light was an old man in flowing gold-and-white robes, sitting on a throne-like chair with two huge ivory tusks standing on end at either side. The PM and Mrs. Fraser sat beside him and he broke some Kolanut with them, which is a traditional symbol of hospitality in Nigeria.'

Afterwards the Australians were taken to a Garden Party in Ibadan held by the local military governor in his elegant grounds. 'We were given a very English afternoon tea under a marquee and there were speeches and the microphone wouldn't work—as microphones inevitably *never* work—and there was lots of humming and hawwing and the PM stamping his feet over the delay.

'On the way back from Ibadan we drove in a convoy along two-lane highways—military roads, apparently,' said Amanda. 'On the outskirts of Lagos there were cyclone and barbed wire fences either side of the highway and crowds of people lined the fences to watch our convoy pass. Now I'm not sure exactly what happened because I was in a car a fair way back, but two people climbed over the fence to cross the road. The convoy was right upon them.

'The first one made a dash between the motorcycle outriders and the first vehicle—and just got through. But the second person, a young girl, was a second slower and was knocked down by the soldier on his motorcycle. The whole convoy screeched to a halt. We were told not to move, to stay in our cars, it was very tense. A few minutes later we all sped on again.

'I heard later that the girl was only injured and had been taken off to hospital for treatment. But the policeman who hit her had been thrown from his cycle and had broken his leg. But apparently he clambered immediately back on to his cycle again, ignoring the pain, and rode another mile down the highway before stopping for help because he was scared of what the crowd might do to him. Mrs. Fraser was pretty shaken by the incident. We all were.'

The Australian party flew on to Lusaka in Zambia on July 31 for the start of the Commonwealth Heads of Government Conference. 'Lusaka airport was crowded with people from all around the world arriving for CHOGM,' Amanda told me.

'There were planes landing continually, and you'd be saying "Oh, there's Mrs. Thatcher's plane!" and, "look, the Indian PM has just arrived!" and, "is that the Canadians?" At the same time you were bombarded by music and colour and the continual movement of a troupe of Zambian dancers who were performing on the other side of the concourse outside the terminal. It was really exciting—but again security was very tight.'

In Lusaka the Frasers and most of the other HOG's were housed in the Mulungshi Village, a cluster of small villas within a compound wall surrounding the conference centre, Mulungshi Hall. The complex had been built for a conference of Non-Aligned Nations in 1970. Andrew Peacock, the Minister for Foreign Affairs and Vic Garland, the Minister for Special Trade Representations, stayed at the Australian High Commissioner's residence, and most of the Australian travelling staff and press were billeted in hotels.

'I was in a hotel which was brand new, probably built for the event,' Amanda said. 'All the staff were enthusiastic and really trying to do their best, although they were obviously very inexperienced and had never served in a restaurant before. There were a few behind the scenes nasties, like the staff being searched every day when they arrived and when they left the hotel. There were severe shortages of some household items in Lusaka at the time. I remember thinking one day, "I'm sure I opened a cake of soap this morning, I wonder where it is?"'

The 22nd Commonwealth Heads of Government Conference opened the next day, Wednesday August 1, 1979. Forty-one nations participated. The host, President Kaunda of Zambia, made the opening address and Malcolm was given the honour of making the speech-in-reply.

He told the conference that time was running out for finding a solution to the problems of southern Africa and that it was vital to recognise and build on areas of agreement rather than be dominated by negative aspects. 'Formidable as the differences on some issues are I believe that, as far as those of us present are concerned, they are differences about means and timing, not about ends.' He emphasised that no-one wanted a solution through slaughter and bloodshed. 'As to what happens next that is not in the lap of the gods, it is to a very large extent in our laps. Time is running out and we may not have such an opportunity again.'

Mulungshi Hall was a big, rather bland-looking building set in the middle of a paddock area. 'From the outside it could have been a technical school in Victoria. The architecture looked the same. But inside it was like a mini-United Nations. People of all colours, all sorts, all dress were dashing up and down the corridors, collaring one another, discussing so and so and his proposal, and such and such a decision, and resolution a, b, and c and really shouldn't it come to *this* conclusion? It was a hive of activity. Buzz buzz buzz.

The Conference room itself was a large room with dark brown woodgrain walls, bright gold carpet and a huge oval table where all the HOG's sat around in strict alphabetical order, with one or two advisers seated behind. Behind them hanging from the gallery above were the flags of each nation. The press were in a different area and weren't allowed to mix. They were on a restricted pass, so-to-speak.

The first night of the Conference the Australian delegation attended a dinner given at the State House by the Queen. 'The State House was a grand old colonial building with a huge gravel driveway and enormous columns and entrances,' Amanda said. 'Everything was done in a manner more English than the English—by black people proudly wearing their traditional national dress. It made such a contrast— the many aspects of colonial life still preserved and enjoyed by everybody and on the other hand a very strong tribal tradition being asserted.'

Each day Tam participated in a program of activities arranged for the wives. They were entertained by Mme. Kaunda, wife of the President of Zambia, at the State House, taken to art and craft exhibitions, drama and dance, the Munda Wanga botanical gardens and even given a game of golf. Everywhere they went security was all-pervading and strictly enforced. 'Mrs. Fraser had a little security officer called Mabel who went everywhere with her. She looked like a little girl guide.

She was a young trainee policewoman brought in from Victoria Falls to help out over the conference and she was very inexperienced. So Mrs. Fraser took her under her wing and used to help her along—show her what to do, where to stand, how to keep guard, etc. Mabel took her job very seriously and was terribly protective, but she was very young for the job.'

One day when Tam returned to the Mulungshi Village from a round of golf for some reason there was no police car following her official car as usual. As she was driven in through the main gate the guards at the entrance stepped forward, brandishing their machine guns threateningly, and signalling her car to stop. Mabel, sitting beside her, went rigid with fright and stared straight ahead through the windscreen. 'Who are you? What do you want?' demanded the guard. As Mabel was in charge no-one else liked to interfere, but she was so paralysed with fear she couldn't answer. Eventually an Australian security officer who was also accompanying them got out of the car, went over to the guard and straightened the matter out.

On Saturday August 4, while some of the HOG's were absorbed in 'private bilateral discussions', Tam and Amanda (plus the ubiquitous Mabel) flew down to Victoria Falls with some other CHOGM representatives. 'There were lots of people there, a crowd of the local people from Victoria Falls gathered around to see the overseas visitors, and the interesting thing was that when Mrs. Fraser was presented to some of them, they said: "Fraser? Fraser? Ah—Malcolm Fraser? Mrs?" and she said "Yes, I'm Mrs. Malcolm Fraser." "Ah, Malcolm Fraser—he our friend! He our friend!" and the word flashed around the crowd to the people in the back row, to the people behind and beyond: "Malcolm Fraser! She! Mrs. Malcolm Fraser! Her! Her!" How they knew what had been going on in Mulungshi Hall we never knew, but somehow word had filtered through.'

The next night, Sunday August 5, the Australian delegation hosted a dinner for all the Heads of Government and their spouses at the temporary Australian

High Commission. 'It was an informal sort of bar-
becue,' said Amanda. 'We had flown Australian wines
over in the hold of the VIP 707 and food as well to
make it a truly authentic Australian evening. The High
Commission's grounds were very suitable, with wide
lawns and lovely old trees, and there were tables spread
out for people to sit at while they had their dinner.

'The guests arrived and drinks were served and Mrs.
Fraser was rushing around making sure everyone was
happy and being looked after—but the drinks seemed
to go on and on and people were starting to wonder
when dinner was going to be served?

'Then suddenly a great whisper flew around the
party, a sort of buzz that Something Big was happening, nobody knew what, but it was a tremendous
undercurrent of excitement. What transpired of course
was that Mrs. Thatcher had arrived late and was very
upset that the agreement on Zimbabwe (Rhodesia)
worked out that weekend in informal sessions had
somehow been leaked to the press. She insisted that
it be approved immediately—or she threatened to
withdraw her support. So the Secretary-General Sonny
Ramphal called the lead players together—U.K. Foreign Minister, Lord Carrington, Mrs. Thatcher, Our
PM, Julius Nyerere of Tanzania and Michael Manly
of Barbados among them—and convened a session of
the Conference. The agreement on Zimbabwe, giving
independence within the Commonwealth and setting
up a system of Governments was approved there and
then.'

The Conference ended three days later. Its final
communique listed other initiatives taken by the member delegations, such as help for communication problems in developing countries and a declaration on
racism. But as Malcolm said on the final day as he and
Tam flew off to visit a game park before leaving for
home, the rest was 'a bit anticlimatic after the agreement on Zimbabwe.'

As a postcript, two years later a pianist friend of
mine called Sally Mellor happened to be travelling
through Zambia en route to a concert tour of Zim-

babwe and when she presented her passport for inspection at the border the young Zambian policewoman who stamped it looked at her, and said: 'Oh, you Australian? Australians are wonderful people! My best friend she is Australian! Perhaps you know her? Her name is Mrs. Tamie Fraser!'

Chapter 14
AUSTRALIANA FUND

On Sunday, October 29, 1979, The Lodge was opened to the public for the first time. 7000 people trooped through the main reception rooms downstairs while the Prime Minister lay in his bed upstairs 'feeling absolutely bloody' with pleurisy and pneumonia.

'Poor Mal,' said Tam. 'The Wednesday before the open day the window cleaners came, but unfortunately no-one remembered Malcolm's bedroom windows were open—we'd been giving him lots of healthy fresh air—and when he was lying there in bed a stream of cold water from a high pressure hose poured all over him. He got up and shut the window and abused everybody on the 'phone, and thought it was all finished. But for some reason another group of window cleaners came the next day—and it all happened again!'

When Tam first moved into The Lodge she was surprised to find that it was regarded by most people as a personal perk of the Prime Minister. Her aim was to change that perception and have the public regard it as belonging to the nation so that the nation would look after it and be proud of it. The open day at The Lodge (and Government House, Yarralumla) was the culmination of that philosophy and the product of 18 months' hard work by the Official Establishments Trust, the Australiana Fund—and Tam herself.

The Australiana Fund (with the help of the National Trust) was in charge of running the day but its President, not wanting to be on exhibition herself, kept out of sight for the duration. But journalist Jennifer Byrne was there and wrote in *The Age*:

> In droves they came crunching the gravel and trampling the grass and filling the house with the pitter-patter of a thousand sensible shoes.
>
> It was Open Day at The Lodge and the big man's health problems were insufficient to deter the curious from the treat promised them—the first close-up, public look at the boudoir of power.
>
> Queues snaked around the Prime Ministerial block, waiting up to two hours. Lots of middle-aged to elderly ladies, ankles swelling with the wait, and various excited others, from the sickbed must have sounded like so many chattering jackdaws.
>
> Kids romped in the Sunday sun while National Trust 'guardians' told the gawkers inside the story of such diverse national treasures as carved, silver-mounted emu eggs (gross, but maybe they grow on you), Chippendale chairs and the use of 'those silver things with holes in them'—sugar shakers.
>
> 'They're not very interested in the furniture,' said one slightly peeved guardian. 'What's really rivetting them is the setting of the dining table—90% of them are asking questions and most of them are about why the soup spoons don't match.'
>
> Yesterday's historic baring of The Lodge was organised by the Australiana Fund . . . What it probably did, one assumes inadvertently was whip up a pretty strong sympathy vote for the ailing Prime Minister, the reason being that the fund declared open day at Government House in Yarralumla at the same time. None of the crowd of about 7000 visitors, bussed efficiently between the two residences, could fail to notice the difference.
>
> The Lodge, to take the kindest view, is a well-turned out family home, of the house and garden style. The rooms are about the same size as those in any pleasant suburb and the ceilings droop low.
>
> The garden is lovely, hung with fragrant wisteria and those buxom white pom-pom flowers. The tennis court is attractive. The pool needs a clean.
>
> That's perhaps a little rough as there's a certain charm about the place with its black and white hacienda facade and stripey awnings. But it's not a patch on Yarralumla's vast rooms and powder-blue tranquility.

Maybe so, but The Lodge has changed a great deal. Chris and I returned there for a few days in the winter of 1979 and we noticed a vast difference from our previous visit. The renovations to the staff quarters had been completed and the main reception rooms done up in soft oatmeal colourings which at last gave them a feeling of unity and space.

'Where are the famous turned-around curtains?' I asked, as Tam was showing us around. When she had first moved into The Lodge there was very little furniture so she had had to use her own sofa and chairs in the drawingroom. The curtains there were very pretty, a soft pink with green flowers and leaves on them, but they clashed with the new suite and so, with the current austerity measures of the time uppermost in her mind, Tam took to the floral curtains with her sewing machine, turning them inside-out, so that their pleasant if uninspired off-white lining now faced the room. 'No-one really realised,' said Tam. 'They looked perfectly tidy and did the job in the interim, although they looked a bit strange from the outside at night when people drove up and pink shadowy flowers showed through from the light inside.'

Now however there were handsome new curtains which reflected the same soft biscuit colour of the rest of the furnishings. Australian paintings hung around the walls—Tucker, Nolan, Boyd, Blackman, Drysdale—which Tamie had managed to "borrow" from the National Gallery. Seeking that elusive sense of history she so desired she had also scrounged around in the national archives and found some historical bits and pieces, such as a collection of cutlery and a Visitors' Book belonging to Stanley Bruce, a trowel of Billy Hughes, and an inkwell which was used for the signing of the first leases sold in the national capital on December 2, 1924. She had these, plus many photographs of past Prime Ministers, out on display.

But the main difference to The Lodge was the result of the work of the Australiana Fund, set up to encourage direct public participation in the acquisition of the finest Australian works of art of all kinds for the four official establishments—Government House, Admiralty House, Kirribilli and The Lodge. The Fund is non-political, self-governing and raises all its own funds. It is administered by a Council made up of members from the seven states and the Australian Capital Territory.

The Council delegates much of the day-to-day running of the Fund to an executive committee which reports to the full council. There is an acquisitions committee which considers the historic or artistic worth of each purchase or donation to the Fund, and a finance committee. 'Dame Helen Blaxland was our first Chairman, a woman of great knowledge and charm,' said Tam. 'And the wife of the current PM is President.'

The idea for the Australiana Fund came from the Americana Fund which was set up by Jacqueline Kennedy to furnish Blair House (the President's Guest House in Washington) and The White House. 'Those two buildings are living museums,' said Tam. 'They are packed with historical treasures and the American people are very proud of them. I was so impressed when I went there in 1976 that it gave me the idea that perhaps something of the same sort could be done here.

'I talked to a lot of people and eventually it was set up under the auspices of the Official Establishments Committee, but as a completely separate body. Official Establishments do have a say in where the pieces are placed and also in what is required—so that instead of the Australiana Fund buying three sideboards and 17 diningroom tables, they buy a card table or a round tea-table or perhaps a secretaire or whatever—and build up a collection of furniture which is really needed, but will also enhance those residences which belong to the nation.

'After all the furore about the plates, I was worried, extremely worried in the beginning, that people would say, "Oh, look! Now she's trying to furnish The Lodge with everyone else's money!" and be catty about it. But I kept making the point that this is not my house—we're only tenants here! In fact the idea

brought a marvellous response from all sections of the
public as well as the press and I was delighted,' said
Tam.

In February, 1978, The Australiana Fund appointed
John McPhee as its fine arts director and began comb-
ing the nation for treasures. Tamie toured the country
giving speeches in its support. 'The public was invited
to donate art works and pieces of furniture or just
plain, good old cash to enable the fund to purchase
any pieces it considered worthy. For instance, take
a look at this sideboard,' said Tam, leading us into the
newly-extended dining-room of The Lodge. 'This
sideboard was found in Hobart and it's very special.
It was made about 1820 from Tasmanian cedar although
the escutcheons and the paterae here are made from
another unidentified wood. And note the brass bands
around the top of the legs and the brass castors. It's
of Sheraton influence and very rare. The Australiana
Fund committee chose it for The Lodge diningroom
and John Fairfax Ltd. and a member of the Fairfax
family donated the money to buy it.'

'What sideboard were you using before?' I asked.

'Ours!' said Tam.

Sitting on the sideboard was an elegant silver hot
water kettle, burner and stand. 'That was donated to
the Fund by Mrs. Alan Lendon from Adelaide,' said
Tam. 'It goes with a silver tea and coffee set and was
made by Jochim Wendt, the Danish silversmith who
emigrated to Australia in 1854. It bears the initials and
crest of the Rymill family.'

The front hall contained other Australiana Fund
additions: an elegant Regulator clock, longcase type,
made in about 1830 of mahogany veneer and an 1840
cedar tilt-top tea table with a centre column on a tri-
form base, both excellent examples of early Australian
furniture making.

In the drawing-room our attention was arrested by
an amazing pendulum clock which sat on one end of
the mantlepiece above the fire-place. Its feature was
a wonderfully alert-looking bronze kangaroo about
30cm high holding the lacquered brass pendulum in

its mouth. At the other end of the mantle-piece was a terra-cotta bust of Edmund Barton sculptured by Nelson Illingworth.

Chris was drawn to the handsome colonial cedar bookcase, which contained elaborately carved emu eggs mounted on silver. The centrepiece was an egg carved with shipping scenes within a heart shape and featuring a kangaroo, a cockatoo, an emu and a kookaburra around the rest of its perimeter. It was set in electroplated silver in the shape of a fern tree with enormous fronds, under which an aboriginal figure made of brass was throwing a boomerang at a kangaroo.

Another emu egg in the collection was suspended from an arch decorated with electroplated floral sprays, an emu and fern finial, and mounted on a wooden base.

'They're turn-of-the-century Australiana,' said Tam, rather haughtily.

'They're turn-of-the-stomach Australiana!' said Chris, laughing.

As part of their Open Lodge philosophy the Frasers entertained as broad a cross-section of people there as possible. 'We tried to get the people of Canberra involved as well as the wider community and we invited representatives from service clubs, businesses, banks, shops, migrant groups, the Aboriginal land council, the diplomatic corps, artists, school principals and Red Cross.

'We heard back on the grapevine later that they all thought we wanted something from them! But in fact all we were trying to do was include them as representatives of their community in the life of The Lodge. The Carlton football premiership team came, groups of Girl Guides, bus loads from old peoples' homes would come for afternoon tea and we would show them around, plus lots of school children.'

Shortly after the Australiana Fund open day at The Lodge, Tamie threw a children's party. 'I felt we should do something in our official capacity to mark the International Year of the Child and as everyone else seemed to be doing intellectual things for the children I thought it would be nice to give a real old-fashioned children's party, with balloons and streamers and jelly cakes and clowns. If I could've had fairies, I'd have had them too! We invited every primary school, including centres for the disabled, from in and around Canberra to send representatives and they accepted with great enthusiasm.

'The day dawned with showers and we thought oh dear, what shall we do if the rain sets in? It was mid-November and we'd been banking on a fine day. All morning we watched the weather, was it going to be fine or wet? The forecast was indeterminate. At twelve o'clock I said we had to make a decision—there was no way we could fit 500 children inside The Lodge—should we move the party to the Albert Hall? People said that would be so disappointing for the children as the whole point of the party was to come to The Lodge, and so if the weather was going to be all right they should still be allowed to come.

'I said you can't move 500 afternoon teas and fantas and thickshakes from one place to another and then back again. I am a country girl, I said, and I think it is going to pour!

'So everything was moved to the Albert Hall, and for the next two hours the sun shone brightly and everyone was grumbling at me. Then, just as the buses were about to drive in the front gates, down came the rain—in buckets! The buses drove up to the front door and I jumped on each one and said, "Children, I'm terribly sorry about the rain. We'll have to go to the Albert Hall, but you can drive around and look at the garden." Then I jumped on the last bus and off we all went.'

'The lucky ones on that occasion were the ones in wheel chairs! The others sat squeezed into rows shoulder to shoulder throughout the hall and we had to pass the cakes and lamingtons and sweets and soft drinks and God-knows-what up and down the lines. Dominic and His Troupe came to entertain the children and they were marvellous. They sang and danced and mimed and played games, with all the children

joining in. Obviously it wasn't the first time the troupe
had encountered a rainy day, a group of fraught grown-
ups and too many children for the size of the venue!
Amanda Derham was there too and some Lodge staff
and they were all marvellous. I think the children
really enjoyed it,' said Tam.

Each year Malcolm gave a series of dinners for the
editors of major newspapers. 'He thought it might
improve Communication,' said Tam. 'He saw it as a
chance to give the press some background for their
better understanding of why certain decisions were
being reached. Malcolm felt an interchange of ideas
should be constructive. Mind you, I don't know that
it was!

'One year we had been to Alice Springs just before
one of these editors' dinners. We had visited an aboriginal settlement at Papunya. Nosepeg, the Head Man
for the Pintubi people was there, and so was Charlie
Perkins, and as we walked around the camp Charlie
said: "Look! This is what my people eat!" as he kicked
the empty baked bean cans and potato chip packets
and sweet wrappers with his toe in the desert dust.
"We used to live well," he said. "We were properly
nourished off the land. We used to have all sorts of
wild fruits—bananas, tomatoes, onions, figs." I said,
"How did you get your sugar?" He told me there are
big honey ants in central Australia with a bulb on the
back. You clasp them by the head and you bite the
bulb, and beautiful honey runs out. It is quite delicious. I asked him to find me one, but it just wasn't
possible at that particular moment, so he said he would
get some for me.'

Tam thought no more about it until, some time
later, she received a little packet of goodies from central Australia, containing all the wild fruits. 'There
were little wild bananas, tomatoes, and wild onions.
I'd have loved to see the plants they came from. Among
them was a jar of honey ants, which, needless to say,
had all died—drowned in their own honey. I didn't
realise the aborigines ate them fresh, but I tasted one
or two and they were still quite delicious. As Malcolm

The Frasers relax at breakfast with newspaper reports of the Liberal Party's 1977 election win . . .

. . . but life is not without drama and dissent. A grim placard greets the Frasers as they attend a Russian ballet performance.

Dancing into the night after the 1980 election victory.

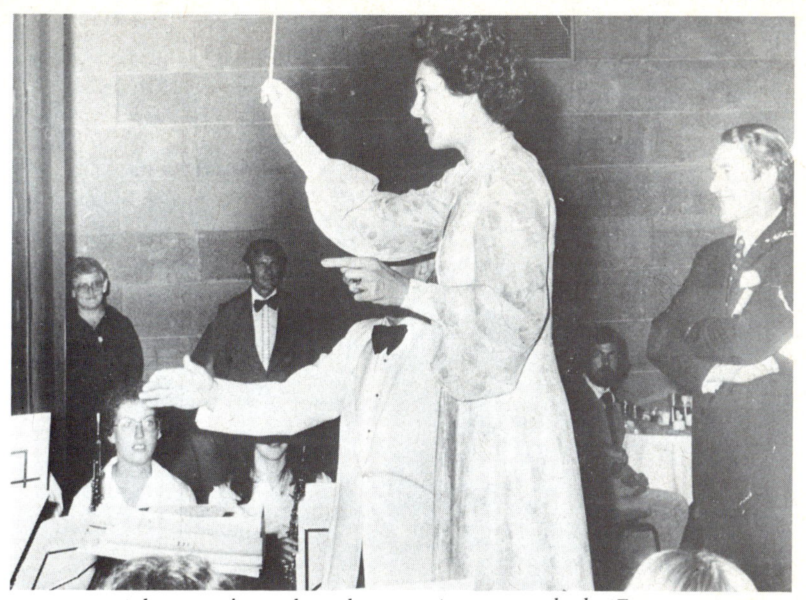

A bemused youth orchestra tries to match the Fraser tempo of Waltzing Matilda.

Prize giver and escort at the Ballarat and Queen's Anglican Junior Grammar School.

Relaxation at Nareen as Malcolm and Tamie Fraser entertain a party of visitors.

Tamie Fraser does her bit to clean up Australia.

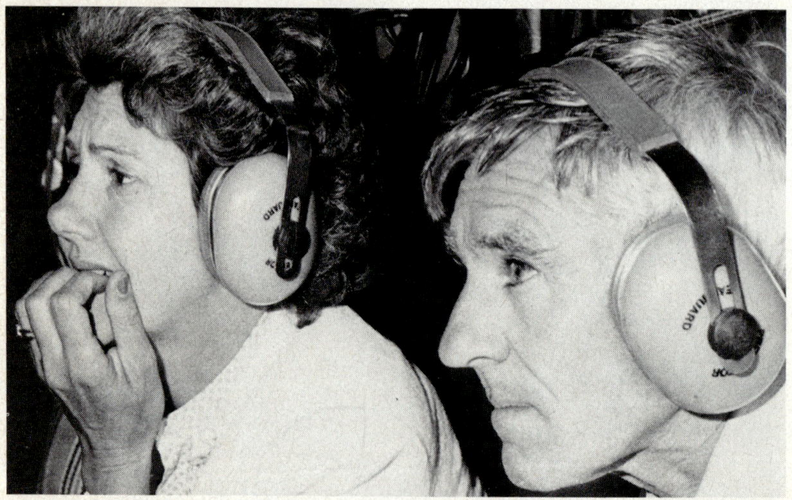

The bushfires of Ash Wednesday rocked the nation during the election campaign of 1983. Tamie Fraser and Liberal Minister Tony Street joined the firefighters in the Waringal Shire, Victoria.

*Malcolm Fraser escorts the Queen at the CHOGM
conference in Melbourne.*

*An animated discussion with President Reagan at a White
House dinner.*

*Tamie Fraser goes electioneering in the Flinders
bi-election of November, 1982, and meets Jacqui Rogers
at the Sorrento pre-school centre, Victoria.*

The result in Flinders – a K.O. victory over Bill Hayden.

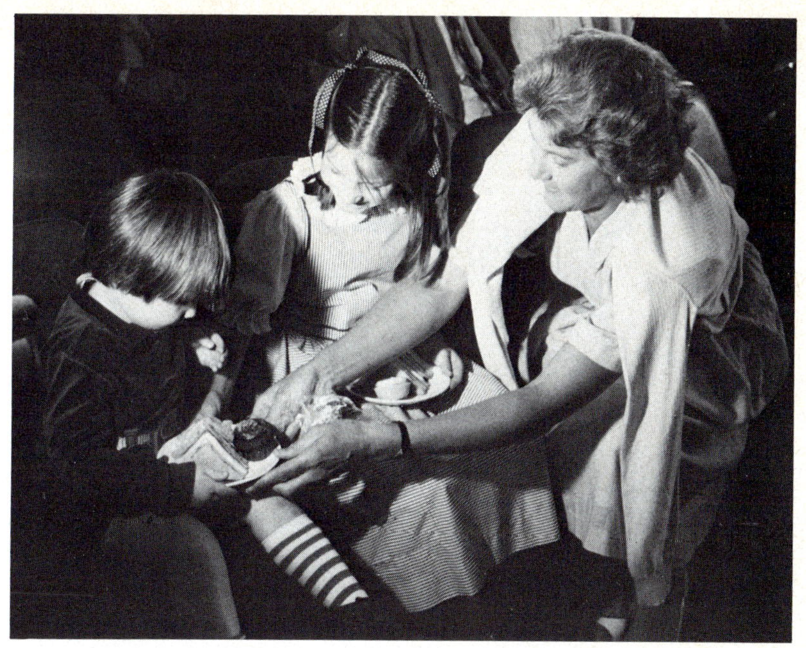

Political life goes on – at a reduced scale. Tamie Fraser acts as 'babysitter' for the children of the new member for Wannon, David Hawker, at his election campaign opening in 1984.

The Lodge, Canberra. Residence of Australian Prime Ministers.

*Malcolm Fraser with his mother at the launching of a
book of his speeches in 1986.*

was having some editors to dinner that night—and the newspapers had been particularly righteous during the last fortnight, I thought what better idea than to serve them the honey ants on their ice-cream—which I did!'

Another day Harry Butler, the naturalist, came to The Lodge. 'He was always finding things under stones, and as the press were coming I thought we must give him something to find under one of our stones at The Lodge! I bought a rubber snake from a toy shop—one of those trick ones that look so lifelike—and wedged it under a rock down by the fishpond. We led Harry off down there with all the reporters and cameramen following along the path behind him, and for a moment I didn't think he was going to notice my snake. So as we passed by I glanced down at the stone, and said: "Oh! Goodness me! What can that be?"

'Harry went straight down on his hands and knees to examine it and I bent down beside him and whispered: "Better take a good look at it, Harry." "Oh no, you wouldn't!" said Harry, groaning. But he played along marvellously. He threw his hat down then grabbed the snake out from under it without a second glance, and announced to the press: "This, ladies and gentlemen, is a Tamie-hoax snake!"'

When Chris and I were staying at The Lodge that winter the Frasers held one of their regular dinners, described in their diaries as "Dinner for Invited Guests" which I thought rather quaint.

The biggest challenge of the night was working out the seating, and Tam and Amanda tackled the task together that morning. 'There's a seniority list for diplomats and civil servants etc. which comes out every year and is signed by the Governor-General— that's the easy part,' said Amanda. 'It's when you get outside that list that the problems start. For instance, should a captain of industry have seniority over a press baron? A medical knight over a knight of the arts? A QC over a PhD? To some it's very important and if you get it wrong people can be very upset and of- fended. But if you do it right it often results in the most boring dinner parties because the same people, due to their set places on The List, have to sit next to each other night after night at different parties!'

The night we were there the dinner guests included a Governor of the Reserve Bank, the head of the Australian Opera, two cabinet ministers, a pollie, an advertising executive, a doctor, a company director, a stockbroker, and two farmers—us!

'Tam! How do we rank?' asked Chris. 'I'll be watching very carefully to see where farmers rank in that list!' and a good deal of irreverence was involved in arranging the seating that night. I do not intend to divulge where eventually we were placed and I am trusting all the other guests have forgotten.

'But everyone needs to see their friends,' said Tam, 'and when you're in The Lodge you need to see them more than ever.' Over the years the Frasers had made many friends outside politics, people from the farming community around Canberra, and these they loved to entertain at The Lodge.

Bill and Dimity Davy were such friends, and Dimity told me one day about an occasion when she and her children went there to lunch, taking with them an English girl who had just arrived out in Australia. 'This girl had had a very unhappy time at school and all sorts of problems,' said Dimity, 'and to cap it off her father had just been killed. We were trying to look after her and put her back on her feet, so Tam said bring her in to see us, because young Hugh was there at the time.

'So off we went, and everyone was being very careful and kind because she was so fragile. Malcolm arrived back just as we were going in to lunch, knowing nothing of the situation, and as we all sat down this dear girl, struggling to make polite conversation, said to him: "Tell me, Mr. Fraser, what do you do?"

'There was a sort of stunned silence, and I looked at Tamie and Tamie looked at Malcolm and Malcolm looked at the girl. Then he smiled and said rather wistfully: "Oh me? I'm really a part-time farmer."'

Chapter 15
LEAD ON, LIBERAL!
ELECTION '80

On October 18, 1980, a federal election was held on the due date for the first time since 1972. In this election the main issues were never the main issue. The opinion polls were. In this election Malcolm, tipped to lose, made his famous remark: 'There's only one poll that counts!'

I remember so clearly the days leading up to the 1980 election because, however astonishing it might sound, fate gave me a tiny role to play. Fate, and my sisters combined, that is.

At the start of the campaign there was no passion out in the electorate. In fact there was scant interest at all. As Peter Cole-Adams wrote in *The Age*: 'Neither in the artificial and incestuous world of Canberra, nor in the country at large, is there any sense of excitement—the sense of imminent change, not just of government but of national directions—that accompanied the poll of 1972.

'Nor are the politicians going to the hustings in an atmosphere of scandal, political crisis and constitutional conflict as they did in 1974 and 1975 and even, to a lesser degree, in 1977.

' . . . As they prepared to escape from Canberra, a surprising number of parliamentarians were admitting that they think the whole campaign will be rather a bore . . .'

Malcolm opened his campaign at the Moorabbin Town Hall with a pledge of continued strong and responsible economic management, and careful planning to harness the potential benefits of the impending resources boom. Bill Hayden, the new leader of the Labor Party, delivered his policy speech at the Greek Community Centre in South Brisbane, slamming the government's record on unemployment, and promising tax cuts, a petrol-price freeze and six broad programmes to reverse the decline in family living standards.

But who's going to pay? responded the coalition.

Yawn, yawn, sighed the electorate.

Then came the first opinion polls and a shock for all. *"Labor Well Ahead!"* was the headline. 'If a Federal election had been held last weekend, Labor would have won comfortably!' said The Age poll of December 4. Suddenly the race was on.

'Yes, we knew we were in trouble,' said Tam. 'After all those years of campaigning you learn to sense how things are going, how people are feeling, and most importantly how people perceive *you* are feeling, about the campaign. It's the little things that show it most clearly. I remember in that campaign Malcolm and I were in Canberra visiting a shopping centre and there were people gathered around to wish us well and as we walked through the crowd we were shaking hands with everyone.

'I shook hands with old ladies and young men and little children, and when I came to a tailor's dummy—you know me, I couldn't resist!—I shook hands with it as well. But the press next day reported it as a mistake, an accident. They didn't see that I *meant* to shake the dummy's hand—to have a joke! Lighten the atmosphere a bit! They took my action as the bumbling error of an over-wrought campaigner. And I knew from that moment that we had a real fight on our hands.'

On Friday, October 10, a special dinner had been organised in Hamilton by the Wannon branch of the Liberal Party at Alexandra House to celebrate Malcolm's 25 years in Parliament as their local member. The function had been arranged months beforehand so when the election was called it was simply absorbed into the PM's campaign itinerary. A few days before this dinner my sister Eda rang up and said: 'Tam says we're in trouble! The campaign's floundering. It's running flat. Nothing's funny anymore. We've got to *do* something!'

'But there's nothing I can do,' I said.

'Yes, there is!' said Eda. '*Be funny*! Tamie wants you to make a funny speech at the Alexandra House dinner—the same speech you made at Mal's 50th birthday last May. She says the whole campaign needs a lift! A boost! A shot in the arm! *It needs something funny*!' Oh my God, I thought. 'Tam says you've got to make that speech again and be even sillier than you usually are!'

'But, Eda, I can't!'

'You've got to!' she said. 'And just think of this. There are only two possibilities. Either it'll be a *complete* disaster, or it won't. And if it isn't, then it'll be OK. Now we both know you won't be a *complete* disaster—so go to it!' And that was that.

I shall never forget the dinner at Alexandra House. Tamie and Malcolm arrived looking tired and tense. My parents were away in South Australia which I remember thinking at the time was probably fortunate, but all the rest of the family were there, plus three hundred of the party faithful and the nation's press— and me expected to stand up in front of them all and *be funny*!

After drinks, the guests went to their tables and dinner was served, during which some other speakers said a few words. The audience was warm and responsive and I was comforted to realise that even if I were to stand up and read out the telephone book, they would probably support me. So I sat in silence and waited until I heard my name being introduced. Chris squeezed my hand under the table. Eda murmured: 'Good luck,' and gave me a shove, and as I walked towards the rostrum I heard my brother Hugh call after me: 'Now is the time for all good rellies to come to the aid of the party!'

'Prime Minister, Big Sister, Ladies and Gentlemen ...' I began, squinting in the glare of the television lights and thinking Please God don't let this be a *complete* disaster! 'We are gathered here this evening to celebrate Malcolm's anniversary—25 years in federal parliament. Now traditionally anniversaries are times for giving presents, and tonight the present which I'm giving you, Malcolm, is your 1980 election Victory Speech! (whistles and cheers). On election night when the returns come in, I've not a shadow of doubt that you will be returned with a huge majority, (more whistles and cheers) and you'll have to make a speech of acceptance—a victory speech! Now as you're very busy at the moment with the election campaign I thought it might be a help if I wrote that speech for you, and that's my present tonight!

'And if you're game to use my speech, Malcolm,' I continued, 'instead of your own on October 18, I'm sure it will go down in history alongside those great moments such as Abraham Lincoln's Gettysberg Address, Henry V before Agincourt, Pericles funeral oration—and Sir John Kerr at the Melbourne Cup!

'If you use my speech, Mal, I'm sure it will make you to oratory what Rembrandt is to painting, what Shakespeare is to the theatre, and what Marcel Marceau is to radio!'

The audience was starting to warm up. I stole a quick glance at the PM and noted with satisfaction signs of real amusement. I caught Tamie's eye and she beamed at me. So far, so good. But this was the risky part. I took a deep breath and ploughed on, saying that in the content of this speech I wouldn't presume to change any of the PM's wonderful words and phrases that we have all come to know and love so well (!), but that in the area of delivery I felt the PM should take a more radical approach.

I then suggested Malcolm deliver my speech on election night using a system of Phonetic Punctuation, whereby you punctuate when you speak in the same way that you do when you write.

This system, devised by Danish comedian Victor

Borge, is practically impossible to describe on paper, but it involves making a series of absurd sounds representing the major punctuation marks of the English language: full stop, exclamation mark, comma, quotation marks and (extremely difficult) the question mark. These noises, when combined with a serious speech, sound utterly ridiculous. It would either be hilarious—or a terrible flop.

'Right! Now let's all imagine it's election night,' I went on. 'The Prime Minister and his staff are gathered at the Southern Cross hotel. At five past nine the first returns come in from across the country, and immediately show a marked swing towards the Liberal Party. By nine-thirty the swing is confirmed and strengthening; by a quarter to ten it's obvious Malcolm will have another huge majority, and by five past ten the shattered Labor leadership has conceded defeat!'

By now I could feel my palms beginning to sweat and I was bemused at how many levels a terrified mind can function on at the same time. On one level I was concentrating for dear life on delivering my speech; but on another level I felt completely detached, merely an observer, my mind roving the surroundings and the situation at leisure and noting small irrelevancies like the odd socks on the man at the far left table, a woman further over furtively picking her nose, and how I seemed to have hardly enough breath left at the end of each sentence.

'The Prime Minister comes out to address the nation. Tamie is by his side with a sickly smile. Phillip Lynch is on the other side with a satisfied smile. And just behind them is Andrew Peacock with a Gucci smile! The lights blaze on, the television cameras roll, and the Prime Minister steps forward to address the nation, and this, Malcolm, is what I suggest you say . . .'

With that I launched into a merciless sendup of Malcolm's politispeak punctuated where appropriate by the extraordinary sounds of Victor Borge. The audience simply roared.

When I eventually came to the end I finished with an extra rude noise and went straight over to Malcolm, oblivious of the applause which rolled around me. I knew it must have been the silliest speech ever made in an election campaign, and I suppose my anxiety was written all over my face. Malcolm responded to it immediately in the form of a great big hug.

'It was fantastic!' said Eda, pushing through the crowd to reach me. 'The press were wetting themselves! Falling apart with laughter! And so was Malcolm! Tam's thrilled!'

I scuttled straight back to Balmoral and didn't surface again for the rest of the campaign. But Tam sent me a clipping from the *Sydney Morning Herald* a few days later which had the headline: *Petee Brings Down the House with Speech of the Year*! Apparently it had not been a complete disaster—and as it wasn't a complete disaster, then I guess it must have been okay.

The Liberal campaign started to crank up once more, gather momentum, and charge ahead. The performances improved, the co-ordination improved, the press coverage improved—and the spirit improved! However, the polls were still terrible and Bill Hayden, along with his 'troika' Labor leadership partners Bob Hawke and Neville Wran, was campaigning more strongly than anyone expected. Chipp was chipping away at both. But Malcolm thrives in a crisis, and now he had his ears pinned back, his nostrils flaring and the wind behind him.

But the odds were still the other way. At the end of the final week all but one of the opinion polls were predicting a Labor victory. 'Only a last minute swing can save Malcolm Fraser from suffering the same massive loss of seats that swept the Whitlam Government from power in 1975,' wrote Ann Summers in the Financial Review the day before the election. But that night Eda rang me and said: 'Don't worry, it's going to be okay! Tam says it's looking good! She thinks they've pulled it out of the fire!'

'But what about the polls?' I asked.

'Remember what Mal says—there's only one poll that counts!'

'I think those dreadful polls actually helped us in

the end.' Tam was to tell me later on, after the election. 'At the start of that campaign people were a bit bored by the whole thing. They didn't want to have to think about it, but if they did, they probably felt they wanted us to go on governing, but they thought we needed a bit of a kick in the pants. Malcolm had pulled the country out of a real bog, but some people thought he could have done more, so they thought we'll give him a bit of a fright—sharpen him up a bit. Then the polls revealed that we might actually lose government, so I think at the last moment a lot of people came back to us. That, plus a crash advertising campaign in the last week which brought attention back to the real issues.'

At eight-thirty on election night television coverage of the count began. Brian Courtis wrote in The Age: '. . . First to air with a drum roll at 8.30 pm was Nine Network with Ray Martin of "60 minutes" reminding us it was Caulfield Cup day and 'have we got a race for you tonight. Settle back, he said, enjoy yourself; have fun.

'Over to George Negus who introduced a panel which included Don Chipp, the size seven politician in a size 14 coat. "It's going to be a cliff-hanger, George," Mr. Chipp said, predicting at that stage a Labor win by 4 seats.

'It was early minutes. Andrew Peacock cautiously predicted a Liberal return, Bob Hawke knew differently, court-jester Fred Daly saw it as a five-to-10 Labor majority, political night owl Alan Reid, clutching binoculars like an anxious bookie, backed the Government.'

Watching the count with his mother back at her flat in South Yarra, the PM was quite unable to sit still. Gathered there to be with him were all his family and some close friends, but he hardly spoke to them. He sat down. He stood up. He paced the room. He sat down again. His tension was palpable.

'. . . At 9.24 pm,' wrote Brian Courtis, 'Don Chipp said he now had "a gut feeling the Government wouldn't be tipped out."

'By 10.12pm the Channel 9 panellists had all swung to a win for the Liberals. "Democracy can be bloody cruel," said Mr. Chipp. "What we're doing here is cooly pronouncing death on certain careers."

'Mr. Chipp, at 10.57, was the first to congratulate the new MP Bob Hawke, and at 11.05 the Prime Minister (came) marching through the Southern Cross to claim his prize.'

When Tamie and Malcolm arrived in at the Southern Cross that night they received a resounding cheer from a crowd of jubilant supporters and staff. And at the end of counting everyone—including the Frasers—took to the dance floor and danced their hearts out till the early hours of the morning in celebration.

The coalition had gained what seemed a comfortable majority of 23 seats in the House of Representatives. But the end result was much closer than that. 12 of those seats were won by majorities of only 1.3%. Of 23 seats decided by majorities of 2% or less, 17 were won by the coalition and only 6 to Labor. One political analyst estimated that the margin between victory and defeat had been just 6000 votes.

The way had been steep and rough, the supporting cast were travel-weary and saddle-sore, the leading players exhausted beyond description—but the show was still on the road!

Chapter 16
THE WHITE HOUSE

In the winter of 1981, after dealing with the problems of Andrew Peacock's resignation from the Ministry and the report of the Ministerial Review of Government Functions—in other words The Razor Gang— Tamie and Malcolm flew off to the United States for talks with President Reagan.

At that time President Reagan was still recuperating from a bullet wound he had suffered in a recent assassination attempt, and before she left Tamie caused the family great merriment by announcing that she was going to ask to see his scar.

'But when I actually met President Reagan I felt ashamed and embarrassed for it even having crossed my mind,' Tam told us on her return. 'Because he was so humble about it, and had been so brave. I don't know whether the general public ever appreciated how brave he'd been over the shooting in order to give confidence to the American people, and I just felt when I was actually there that it wasn't something you made jokes about—it was all too real.'

In most countries official welcomes are highly political and designed to indicate the status which exists between the host and the visiting nation at the time. 'In China, for instance, we had been given a TW (tumultuous welcome) because Malcolm was being beastly to the Russians and the Russians were the Chinese's sworn enemies at the time. We were given the Full

Works when we went to America as well because of our stance over the Moscow Olympic Games and support for ANZUS and the American alliance.'

The Frasers were greeted by President Reagan on the lawns of the White House on Tuesday, June 30, 1981. 'The Americans are masters of ceremony and it was all beautifully done,' Tam said. 'There was a plaque to show you where to stand, a little marker on the lawn saying "Mrs. Fraser" or "Mrs. Reagan" or whoever, to ensure that everyone stood in exactly the right positions for press protographs and television.'

Before the welcoming ceremony the Frasers and their party were given a program containing the order of service plus some notes on White House customs:

During the playing of Honors for the President and the Visiting Dignitary, it is customary that White House Guests observe the following:

Stand at attention during the playing of Ruffles and Flourishes (Musical Salute).

Stand at attention during the playing of Hail to the Chief.

During the playing of the National Anthems, salute by placing your right hand over your heart. If gentlemen's hats are worn, the hat is held over the left shoulder with the hand over the heart.

'Yes, we did all that, and it was all very colourful and razzamatazz,' said Tam. 'There were troops on review in wonderful bright uniforms, massed bands playing and the artillery gave a 19 gun salute. Royalty, Presidents and Heads of State always receive a 21 gun salute; Prime Ministers 19. There was an inspection of the guard of honour then the President made a speech of welcome and Malcolm responded.'

After the ceremony the Australian visitors were shown into the Blue Room, a large oval reception room in the White House decorated in the French Empire style chosen for it by President James Monroe in 1817. It looked magnificent, entirely furnished in blue, white and gold. From the middle of the ceiling hung a gilt wood chandelier encircled by acanthus leaves. An Empire motif was featured in gold leaf on the cornice and on the ceiling medallion, as well as in the blue and gold frieze atop the white silk-screen wall paper.

The huge French windows facing out on to the south lawn were framed by blue satin curtains with gold satin vallances. The blue silk on the gilded *begère* armchairs was embroidered with gold in the original Monroe design. The walls were hung with portraits of past presidents—Andrew Jackson painted in 1810 by John Wesley Jarvis, Thomas Jefferson painted by Rembrandt Peale in 1800 (when he was still Vice-President), and an 1859 portrait of John Tyler painted by George Healy.

'It was quite fascinating and we were only too happy to wait there, being wonderfully entertained, while Malcolm went off to the Oval Office for Preliminary Discussions, which really means a little chat, with President Reagan.'

That evening the President and Mrs. Reagan gave an official banquet at the White House in the Frasers' honour. Ninety guests were invited and it was held in the State Diningroom.

This was a magnificent room, modelled on the neo-classical English houses of the late 18th century. It had an ornate white plaster ceiling and cornices, and white-painted oak-panelled walls with Corinthian pilasters and a delicately carved frieze. In the middle of the room hung a huge gilt chandelier and all around there were gilt sconces lighting the walls. The windows were hung with gold silk-damask curtains and the Queen Anne-style chairs covered in gold cut-velvet.

On this occasion the dining table was arranged in the shape of a 'W' with guests seated around all sides, and it was decorated with gold rococo-revival can-delabra and some magnificient *bronze-d'ore* pieces from a gilt service purchased by President Munroe from France in 1817.

'Everything was gleaming white and gold and it was all very sumptuous and grand, but the most striking feature of the room was a very dark and sombre portrait of President Lincoln hanging over the central fireplace. The very plainness of the painting in contrast to its glittering surroundings made it stand out as the focal point of the room. It made such an eloquent statement about how Americans view their Presidency.

'Each time I went to America what impressed me was how much the people there revere their Presidents. There are wonderful memorials in Washington which are world famous to Thomas Jefferson and Abraham Lincoln, statues of them sitting there with their words engraved in the walls around them, quoting the best things that they said in their lives. That seems a wonderful monument to men who have tried to give a lot, and it struck me how we have never really revered any political leader in this country. We've always had the Royal Family for our figurehead, but the Americans shelved the monarchy very early on in their history and I suppose they needed to create another figurehead to admire.

'Americans love heroes, whereas Australians are a bit embarrassed by them, I think. Australians like to cut tall poppies down to size.'

Beneath the portrait of Abraham Lincoln, carved into the mantelpiece, was an inscription from a letter written by John Adams, the second President of the United States, on his second night in the White House in 1797: 'I Pray Heaven to Bestow the Best of Blessings on *This House* and on All that shall hereafter Inhabit it. May none but Honest and Wise Men ever rule under this Roof.'

After an entree of cold salmon and sole Mousse Doria served with Souce Verte and triangles of pita bread, the guests were given Roast Contre-filet of Beef, Tiny Potatoes and Tomatoes Provencale plus snow peas. Then followed Escarole, Bibb Lettuce and Avocado Salad, Brie aux Fines Herbes, plus Frozen Lemon Souffle with fresh Raspberries and assorted Macaroons for dessert. All this was washed down with Trefethen Chardonnay 1978 and Robert Mondavi Cabernet Sauvignon 1974.

After dinner the guests were taken to another room

and entertained by Vincent Dowling reciting stirring highlights from the Great Lakes Shakespeare Festival Production of 'My Lady Luck,' taken from the Life, Times and Works of the Canadian author James A. Brown. Tamie sat next to President Reagan all evening—and has been mad about jelly beans ever since.

When the Frasers were in Washington they stayed at the official visitors' residence, Blair House. The experience made a great impression on them. Built in 1824, Blair House had a distinguished history in the life of the nation long before Franklin Roosevelt acquired it for the President's Guest House in 1942. Situated at 1653 Pennsylvania Avenue within sight of the White House, it has been carefully restored and filled with treasures of Americana: portraits, furniture and furnishings, early china, silver and glass, plus a unique collection of Lincolniana.

'There were leaflets everywhere explaining the story of each item or each section of the house. Apart from being a comfortable and highly functional visitors' residence, it was also a museum and showcase for the finest examples of America's cultural and artistic heritage.'

In America of course security is an integral part of political life, and the security officers assigned to the Frasers were highly-trained professionals dedicated to their job.

'But sometimes they were a little too professional. One evening when we arrived back to our rooms I asked the security man who'd been with me all day please could he tell me the name of our driver.

'I don't know his name, he said.

'But you've been sitting next to him in the car all day!'

'But I'm from Chicago!'

'I don't care where you're from! Here I am all the way from Australia, and we're told you Americans are the best communicators in the world. Yet you don't even say hello to each other! I'm lucky if you mumble Good Morning to me in the mornings! You want to take a good, hard look at yourselves! You simply don't communicate at all!

'Later on that evening when we came down to go out to dinner he shuffled up to me, looking a bit sheepish, and said: "Joe." And the next morning he said "Good morning, Mrs. Fraser!" with a great twinkle in his eye—and we became friends from then on. But I can only presume he was like that because he wasn't used to being treated as a person, only a mobile gun.'

Another day when Malcolm was busy at talks with State Department officials, Tamie went shopping, and thought she had only two security officers accompanying her but soon discovered she actually had 12.

'I was at the lingerie counter of one of the big department stores and as I was being served I noticed that the girl behind the counter kept glancing over my shoulder. I looked around and there were 12 men in raincoats standing just behind me all in very peculiar positions. You can always pick a security officer because he stands so peculiarly and I'm told that's because he keeps his gun in a very peculiar place! Anyway, I took fright and left. It really was a bit much trying to choose your smalls with 12 strange men gazing over your shoulder!'

The Frasers had been to Washington in 1980 to meet President Carter, and also in 1976 as guests of President Ford. 'Gerald Ford was a far better President than his public reputation gave him credit for,' Malcolm told me once. 'He came to power at a very difficult time in the aftermath of Watergate, and he had to make the decision to pardon Nixon—he had no option but to do that.'

When the Frasers were in Washington in 1976 President Ford gave an official dinner at the White House for 200 people in their honour. 'We arrived at the White House at the appointed time and were met by the President and Mrs. Ford and taken upstairs to a private room to have a drink with them while the guests were assembling downstairs,' said Tam. 'The four of us chatted for about ten minutes, I suppose, then an aide came up and said: "Mr. President, the guests are ready now," and we left the room and walked slowly down the big staircase—you know, the one where Sonia McMahon was photographed in *that* dress!—while the band played "Hail to the Chief!" I found it disarming that President Ford seemed so totally unaffected by the grandeur of that music, which is very formal and rousing. He just strolled easily and naturally down the staircase—in a true democratic manner!'

After Tamie and Malcolm had greeted all the guests they walked with President and Mrs. Ford through the floodlit garden to a marquee which had been erected on the east lawn, 'and all along the way our path was lined with violinists playing "Waltzing Matilda", which of course was still being used as our national anthem at the time. And they played it with such a lilt, in waltz time—it was so moving!'

The travelling Australian press were at the White House that night too, and John Hamilton wrote in *The Sun* (Melbourne):

Australian-US relations have been cemented to the tune of 'Dancing Cheek-to-Cheek.'

That's what the Marine Corps dance combo was playing tonight when President Ford swept Tamie Fraser to his arms and whirled her around the dance floor in the White House. At the same time, Prime Minister Fraser was floating past with Betty Ford who was dressed in a cloud of green chiffon.

The Fords threw a party at the White House for the Frasers. The guests of honour and about 200 others were still dancing after midnight. And what a guest list. There was Jimmy Connors and his girlfriend, former Miss World, Marjorie Wallace, Gregory Peck, Rod Steiger and Cyril Ritchard.

John Newcombe, Bruce Crampton and Mr. Fraser's favourite author, Ayn Rand, a large lady in a severe black dress patterned with green flowers, were also there. Prime Minister and author were seen late in the evening in earnest conversation by a marble fireplace under a portrait of Abraham Lincoln.

The evening began at 8pm when guests gathered under

a tent in the Rose Garden of the White House. There was fine food washed down by fine wines, formal speeches and toasts.

It was after dinner that the Americans and Australians let their hair down in what one White House correspondent described as 'the fun party of the year.'

President Ford with Mrs. Fraser on his arm, and Mr. Fraser with Mrs. Ford on his arm, led the way to the Red Room. As a string quintet played outside, the Fords and Frasers sat down to after dinner coffee and liqueurs with Secretary of State Henry Kissinger and Foreign Minister Mr. Peacock.

In the adjoining Blue and Green Rooms the guests mingled. CIA Director George Bush chatted with Admiral James Holloway, Chief of US Naval Operations—perhaps about the successful evacuation of Americans from Lebanon this week.

Two former US ambassadors to Australia—William Battle and Ed Clark, compared notes on Canberra with the present US Ambassador to Australia James Hargrove, who flew back to Washington for the Fraser visit. Six Senators and nine Congressmen thrashed out Republican politics. They hunted commitment from the six uncommitted delegates invited by the President to the state dinner.

President Ford called John Newcombe to the Red Room to get some tips on his tennis serve.

Dr. Kissinger kidded Australian correspondents: 'Oh, ho, you are the tough Australian press who gave my wife such hell when she came to your country?'

The ice began to melt. Mr. Ford led the way to the East Room of the White House. Mr Jon Spong sat himself in dinner jacket and ruffled shirt at a huge grand piano, and Mr. Ford introduced the entertainment for the evening, baritone Sherrill Milnes, from the New York Metropolitan Opera.

Mr. Milnes sang arias from Gounod and Mozart that set the three huge crystal chandeliers shivering with the resonance. Mr. Kissinger, sitting in the front row next to Mrs. Fraser, began to nod off.

There was time to notice little things as the baritone continued singing.

Little things like the fact that Gregory Peck wears built up shoes and old blue socks and an ancient dinner jacket. That Tamie looked superb in a simple white gown with pearls and that President Ford was beginning to nod off, too.

That is, until Mr. Milnes completed his performance with a moving rendition of 'Shenandoa' and the Gettysburg Address of President Lincoln set to music. Then President Ford said: 'Let's all move into the next room. Let's dance and enjoy ourselves.'

Which we all did.

Mr. Peacock skipped around the floor with one of the niftiest dancers of all time—the President's new chief of protocol, Shirley Temple Black, in a blue dress with a red sash.

White House photographer David Kennerly bopped with his latest beautiful girlfriend Paula Ahalt.

The French champagne flowed.

'Come on, Mrs. Ford,' said the world's most powerful man. 'Let's dance.' They did, cheek to cheek. So did Malcolm and Tamie.

Chapter 17
ROYAL WEDDING

The Royal Wedding caused just as much excitement out in the country as it did in the cities, and living near a place called Balmoral (and owning a pet Corgie!) I felt a particular responsibility not to let the occasion pass unnoticed. So when a friend on a nearby property invited me to a celebratory women's luncheon, I accepted with alacrity.

I arrived at her homestead at the appointed hour and was greeted by the smiling faces of Prince Charles and his bride beaming from a giant tea towel pinned to the front door. Beside the front step there was a polo stick and a pair of long leather riding boots. A riding helmet sat casually in a tub of flowering plants nearby.

We drank to the happy couple's health in copious quantities of champagne, and while we sat around the dining-table for lunch a Royal Wedding record with wonderful stirring pieces like 'Zadok the Priest' and 'Land of Hope and Glory' thundered from the stereo. When 'I Vow to Thee My Country' came on we positively swooned with emotion and with the inevitable 'God Save the Queen' we all solemnly rose without hesitation from our seats and stood to attention mid-chew for the duration. Afterwards we rollicked home to our hard-working husbands and watched transfixed as the whole fairy-tale event unfolded on television.

It is needless to describe therefore my eagerness to hear from Tamie all about The Real Thing. At the earliest opportunity I flashed over to Nareen, sat her down and begged her to tell all.

'Well, I'm sure you all saw more than I did on television! but it was really exciting to be there. The wedding was at midday but we had to leave our hotel at 8.45am all dressed up to the nines—best hat, gloves, shoes, face—the lot. I wore a dress of cream silk with yellow roses, a large cream hat trimmed with yellow, and a matching yellow light-wool coat.

'The crowds were unbelievable and our progress was snail's pace along the Mall. There was an Australian flag on the front of our car and every now and then some Aussies in the crowd would see us and call out: "Gidday, Mal! Gidday, Tamie!"

'Spike Milligan was in the car ahead of us in his morning coat and striped trousers looking very dapper, and he kept jumping out and doffing his hat to the crowd and doing little tricks to amuse them. Then he'd climb back in and we'd all move on, then the traffic would stop again and out he'd pop. The crowd just loved it!

'At one stage some people in a little yellow miniminor drew alongside our car and noticing the Australian flag called out: "Are you the Frasers?" And we nodded vigorously. And they called: "Our daughter's just been to a party with your son in Armidale (NSW)!" And off they sped. And that was so!

'Eventually we reached the Cathedral and joined in the queue of people on the steps waiting to be shown inside. We found ourselves standing between Ted Heath and Harold Wilson, two British Prime Ministers defeated at the polls, and I said to Malcolm—I hope this is not an omen! When our turn came we were led down the aisle of the Cathedral through a sea of beautiful hats; everywhere you looked gorgeous hats, wonderful colours and shapes.

'And then we were shown to our seats. We had the Bahamas on one side and New Zealand on the other,' said Tamie, and rolled her eyes. 'And I don't know if it were an accident or someone in Protocol with a sense of humour, but there was an aisle between us and the Muldoons! We were seated very early, but it didn't seem a long time to wait because there was always something happening, something to see all the time. There was the Ecclesiastical Procession then the Royal Heads of State arrived one by one, all timed like clockwork, then the British Royal Family, the Beefeaters, The Queen's Lifeguards, the Orders of Chivalry &c. &c.—and I noticed many of these people looked extremely old and seemed almost weighed down by their finery, even though they wore it so proudly.

'And all the time there was wonderful music. The woman in front of me, looking frightfully elegant and immaculate, kicked her shoes off under the chair while she was waiting. I suppose they were new and killing her, but it looked rather incongruous!

'Then came the Big Moment—we could tell when Lady Diana was nearing the cathedral because the cheering from the crowds outside grew louder and louder, great waves of cheering rising in a crescendo which finally enveloped us as she entered the back of the cathedral. The congregation rose to its feet and the bride came down the aisle supporting her father on her arm. I nearly wrenched my eye-balls out trying to see as much as possible sideways without actually turning around and I caught a glimpse of white as the bride went past, then eventually I could see a little white speck up at the altar.

'There were masses of crowned heads and assorted royal rellies in all the front seats, then came all the Presidents and Heads of State then us Prime Ministers, so we were about 20 rows back. Mrs. Reagan looked very lonely. President Reagan was still recovering from the assassination attempt so she had come on her own. You would have thought someone could have walked with her down the aisle but she came in all by herself.

'When Kiri Ti Kanawa began to sing I thought it would lift the roof off the Cathedral, it was so beautiful. Afterwards the Kings and Queens filed out of the Cathedral first and I was disarmed to see one member of the Royal Family wearing the same silk as my dress only with pink roses. I thought how small the world has become when you can buy some material in Melbourne and travel to the other side of the world to find the same material—at the Royal Wedding!

'Finally we left the Cathedral and waited on the steps for our car. The traffic and the crowds were unbelievable and a voice shouted from somewhere "Hi Tamie! Hi Mal! Never vote for you, but it's good to see ya here!" and we could see hands waving frantically at us. When after ages our car still hadn't arrived Malcolm suggested we walk instead, so we walked to Guildhall for lunch. The Queen had all the Royals to lunch at Buckingham Palace and the Prime Minister, Mrs. Thatcher, had a luncheon at Guildhall for all the Commonwealth Prime Ministers and other visiting Heads of State.

'We were particularly impressed at the way security was handled the whole day,' Tam went on. 'The British hate to make a big show of anything but security was a real problem as there'd been a scare with the Queen at the Trooping of the Colour not long before. So the police asked the public themselves to keep watch, and on the day the police were laughing and joking with the crowd and yet all the time watching carefully and keeping close control.

'It was masterful but only possible because it was such a wonderful, happy atmosphere. People who had watched the procession from balconies said that the escort guards riding either side of the carriage and the footmen were moving forwards and backwards constantly as the carriage moved along and so there was never a moment long enough for anyone to focus on the royal couple to take aim without the bodies of these guards blocking the view. They moved just enough so that you couldn't get a sighting—and yet just to watch you couldn't tell that they were ever marching out of place. It was so discreet and understated.'

The night before the wedding Tamie and Malcolm had been to dinner at Buckingham Palace and then on to a fireworks display. 'Before I dressed I asked someone, what does one wear to dinner and the fireworks?

I was advised to wear something point-to-point which to me meant a tweed skirt, scarf tied under the chin and a Burberry raincoat—yet that seemed hardly the ticket for dinner at the palace. Malcolm had arrived from Australia only two hours before, landing in a helicopter in Hyde Park just in time to reach our hotel and change before setting off for Buckingham Palace.

'The dinner was amazing. There must have been 200 people there and half the treasures from the Royal Collection adorning the table. Every guest had a title or was head of his or her country. I sat between Lord Hailsham and the Crown Prince of Jordan and they had a violent discussion about affairs in the Middle East, which obviously I can't tell you about. But we felt so honoured to be there representing Australia.

'When dinner was over we all went off and took our seats at the fireworks. There must have been 100,000 people there, and crowds suffocate me, as you know, but no scuffling, no unpleasantness. Everyone had brought their picnic and were having a real night out. It was a wonderful atmosphere. I only saw one woman working. She was dressed in a skin-tight dress of black sequins and her lips were painted scarlet up to her nostrils and out to the corners of her mouth and down to the point of her chin and she was puffing on a cigarette in a long black cigarette holder and leaning against a lamp post.

'The traffic was still unbelievable on the way home and when we'd moved only ten years in ten minutes Malcolm said: "I've been sitting in a plane for 27 hours; I've been sitting at dinner for three hours and I've been sitting at the fireworks for two hours—let's walk!"

It was probably two miles back to our hotel, and as we were striding along through the crowd a little boy suddenly jumped in front of Malcolm and said: 'Excuse me, sir. You look important. Are you important?' Malcolm said sorry, not very. 'Where are you from sir?' Australia, said Malcolm. 'Are you the Prime Minister?' Yes. 'Oh, how nice to meet you sir,' he said, and off he went.

'Then we walked on a bit further and an old and

rather battered campervan came along the road beside us with people on top of it and people hanging out the windows and out of the back as well, and one of them yelled: "Hey! There's our Prime Minister! Hello Mal!" and they stopped and all tumbled off and one of them had a tape-recorder and said he was making a tape of the Royal Wedding to send back to the family in Australia and could he have a pretend interview with the PM. So he walked along beside us saying in a very ABC voice and using all the right journalistic lingo: "Good evening, Prime Minister. Tell me, sir, what are your views *vis a vis* the Royal wedding?" We walked all the way back to our hotel eventually arriving about midnight.'

I drove back to Balmoral and as I pulled up, I remembered Tamie had never actually told me what point-to-point outfit she had worn to dinner and the fireworks. I still don't know.

Chapter 18
AUSTRALIA — THE ELECTORATE

A Prime Minister has for his electorate the whole of Australia, and during their term in office the Frasers visited as much of that electorate as possible. One day I called in at Nareen to find Tam crouched on the floor in the den before a roaring fire, a large map of Australia spread out before her. Into it, she was sticking a vast array of coloured pins.

'I'm marking some of the places we've been since Malcolm became PM,' she said. 'What do you think?'

'It looks like a technicolour porcupine,' I replied. Tam had just returned from a visit to Kalgoorlie where she had been speaking with outback children over the School of the Air. 'It was most fascinating hearing those little voices crackling over the air waves, chatting away to each other despite the immense distances between them. And they are so used to it! They laughed at how bad I was at working the buttons on the radio set but I got the hang of it after a while and we had a great old chat. I asked them about their families and their pets and did they ride horses and did they milk a cow. Just country things. All around me on the walls of the School of the Air were photographs of the children doing their school work. One was writing on his knee, listening to the two-way radio in the front of a landrover; another was sitting out on a back verandah with his dog and his cat; another was working in the kitchen; another was away in some sort of tin shed—it looked like a machinery shed.

'These kids only have half hour a day formal session, so when it comes on their concentration hones in on it to the exclusion of all else. One time we visited an outback station near Katherine in Queensland, landing on the station airstrip in a cloud of dust. As usual we were quite a menagerie, with staff and security, etc. and our invasion must have been rather unnerving for this isolated family. The mother and father coped well but the little children were very shy.

'Then the radio came on with the School of the Air. Suddenly the children forgot their self-consciousness and their shyness, forgot that there was a room full of big politicians from Canberra all covered with red dust. It was total concentration. They listened intently to their teacher and answered her questions. The radio was rather crackly, like those old recordings you hear of the BBC, but coming through the static you could hear a little voice from Thursday Island and an answer from 500 miles south then the teacher coming in again. I found it very moving.'

Being country people themselves, the Frasers were always in demand to open country shows. 'One Spring we flew to Bourke to open a show,' said Tam, sticking a pin into north central New South Wales. 'There was a big crowd gathered at the show grounds there because, well, I suppose Prime Ministers don't come to Bourke every day. I was asked to present the trophy for the best hand-knitted garment while Malcolm judged the best local trade exhibit and as I was moving around the stands two little girls came up to me, and said: "Mrs. Fraser, we think you're just lovely!" and they started following me around. I smiled at them, you know, bared my fangs, from time to time, and after a while they disappeared. But not long afterwards they came back and said: "Mrs. Fraser, we would like to give you a present!" and they presented me with a ring. And I said oh, how kind. This is a lovely ring. And I wedged it on my finger and flashed it proudly for the rest of the afternoon.

'It had sort of bits of red glass in gold and it looked a bit better than the normal kind of ring you get in a cracker or a bubblegum machine, but I didn't really think much about it. Two days later one of Malcolm's security men rang me up and said, 'Mrs Fraser, you know that ring you were given in Bourke—do you still have it? And I said yes, I think it's at the bottom of my handbag. And he said, "Well, do you think you could give it back, it was stolen!"'

At Burketown, a very small and isolated community right up in the Gulf of Carpentaria, Tamie received a vastly different gift. 'Some of the townspeople took Malcolm fishing and they gave us a wing ding party that night. Altogether we had a marvellous time, and when we came to leave we were presented with two baskets filled with little jars of homemade jams and jellies made by the women of the area—all different kinds, and they had put their names on the jars, who had made what. It was one of the nicest gifts we ever received.'

Malcolm's enthusiasm for fishing was well-known, so when the Frasers visited Geraldton on the central coast of Western Australia the local people planned to take them fishing. But there were terrible floods at Carnarvon at the time so they made a tour of inspection of the flood damaged areas instead. 'However, just before we left our hosts presented Malcolm with an enormous snapper, deep frozen, and said they were so sorry they couldn't take him fishing but that as he ate his fish he was to dream of what it would feel like on the end of his line.'

Malcolm did go fishing however when he visited the Northern Territory—only this time he himself, and not the fish, was caught. 'Galarrwuy Yunipingu, the Chairman of the Northern Lands Council, took him fishing in Kakadu National Park,' said Tam, sticking another pin in her map in Arnhem Land in the Northern Territory. 'But apparently it was in an area for blacks only. Someone, some white person, had just been prosecuted for fishing in these same waters and so when he heard about Malcolm's fishing expedition there he got together with the Labor Party and launched a prosecution. No-one realised that the law was written in such a way that a black wasn't even allowed to invite a white to go fishing there as his guest—I think it has been changed since.

'Anyway, the case went to court and the verdict was that the facts were proven, but no conviction recorded!'

I noticed a pin at Emerald on the mid Queensland coast. 'Yes, we went up there to visit Thiess Bros. open cut and underground coal mining operations, then we climbed into a Chinook helicopter and flew on to Norwich Park to watch the Dampier Mining Company blast a new layer of coal at their open cut mine. We stood with the mining company officials back a safe distance waiting and suddenly there was a thunderous BOOM—but only little puffs of dirt came up. They started at one end of the open cut and went all along the bank, poof poof poof and then at last a cloud of dust rose in the air. Cores were put down, so, instead of blowing the overburden sky high they disintegrate the layers just below the surface into rubble so they can be easily scraped off.'

For Tam, the best aspect of travelling around Australia was meeting so many different people. One year the Frasers visited Derby in Western Australia because the PM wanted to discuss the Nunkumbar dispute over oil drilling with the Aboriginal elders who lived there. 'But I talked to the wives. There was a group of them there, keeping their distance, sitting on the ground about 50 yards away from the circle of men, looking on. Now people from remote areas anywhere in the world, whether they are aboriginal, or Eskimo, or Indian or Chinese, people who are very shy and are not used to the world, find a big influx of visitors, especially politicians, rather unnerving. And whereas with city people you can barge up and smile and start chatting away immediately, eye to eye, to draw them out, you find outback people quite different. They don't want to be bombarded by a big, strange woman. You have to take the opposite approach—stand close but not too close and talk into the distance and leave little spaces in your conversation, just take it slowly.

It's communication through sensory measures as much as words. I'd sort of stand slightly apart and gaze off into the distance and say, I wonder if anyone uses the sewing centre that's just been built up here, or that's a lovely new hospital over there—I wonder how many women go there to have their babies? Then I'd pause, and wait and there'd be some shuffling of feet and then someone would say, "Yes, I use the sewing centre." "So, do I," would join in another. "Yes, and I went to the hospital, too," from someone else. Soon they'd get going and become quite chatty and I would learn such a lot from them.'

For Tam factories are the heartbeat of the nation and she travelled all over Australia to visit them. There were pins in her map at Albury (Borg-Warner), Wagga Wagga (Waratah Industries), Launceston (Repco Bearings), Ballarat (Paddle Shoes), Orange (Email), Warrnambool (Fletcher Jones), to name just a few. 'One of the first factories I visited was a glass factory. It was in the heart of a blue ribbon Labor electorate in Sydney and the unions had been pretty toey so I didn't know what sort of reception I would get—nor did the people from the glass factory. There was still that terrible hate thing left over from 1975. I put on a protective overcoat, and helmet and protective goggles and set off with the manager on a tour through the factory. It was terribly hot and steamy and full of loud engine noises and hissing and there was hot, hot molten glass being poured and water all over the floor—the whole thing was really quite nerve-wracking.

'As I walked by, one of the workers came up and started shouting at me. I looked at him and thought, "Oh dear, I wonder what he's saying?" It was all so noisy and I couldn't hear a word. He tried again but I still couldn't hear what he said, but I guessed he was probably being rude so I just nodded and smiled and continued my tour of the factory. At the end of the afternoon he appeared outside, and came up to me, and said: "Mrs. Fraser, you didn't hear a word I said, did you?" I said, to be honest, no, I didn't. Were you being beastly? And he laughed, said: "No, I wasn't!

I was saying welcome to you on behalf of the Glass-
blowers' Union. We were delighted to have you in
our factory!"'

I drew Tam's attention to a pin stuck in Burnie,
Tasmania. 'Oh, yes, Malcolm and I toured that area
one time, and I visited an old people's centre there.
I had a lovely long talk to one dear old man and at
the end of it he looked at me sort of misty-eyed, and
said: "You remind me so much of my dear wife. She
died two years ago. She was 78." I knew he meant
the remark as a compliment, but I shot off for a hair-
do, facial and a manicure the very next day!

'I suppose I've visited hundreds of old people's
centres now, all over Australia, and what always strikes
me is how often they're stuck out on the periphery
of townships. I know they have beautiful views and
invariably lovely gardens, but when you are getting
old I feel it is rather nice to be able to watch the world
pass by—girls in pretty clothes, and young lovers, and
mothers wheeling babies, and children running and
playing—people living their lives. I feel that the whole
concept of putting homes for the elderly out on their
own is wrong. I'd like to see people still in the centre
of their communities rather than on the periphery in
their old age.'

I looked at the map to see if there was a pin stuck
in Townsville, Queensland. There was—but I didn't
mention it. Dale Budd, Malcolm's private secretary,
had already told me about that visit. Malcolm and
Tamie had gone up there to officially open a new
offshore port, Lucinda, and visit the buildings of the
Australian Volunteer Coast Guard Association. 'Now
on these occasions the PM liked his speeches to be
very straight,' Dale told me. 'No slang, no slick remarks, no colloquialisms; and if his speechwriters
sometimes put colloquialisms into his speeches, he was
always reluctant to use them. On this occasion we
arrived at our hotel in Townsville, and the PM and
Tamie sort of disappeared for about twenty minutes
or so into the bedroom to rest and change, then the
PM reappeared, followed a few minutes later by Tamie.

'The PM sat down and started to check through the speech he was about to make. It said how much he was enjoying being in Townsville, that things were going really well, and he was on Cloud Nine. "What's this Cloud Nine?" he demanded. "What's it mean? What's Cloud Nine?" All the staff looked at each other for a moment wondering how on earth to explain, when suddenly from away in the corner, Tamie says: "Darling, Cloud Nine is where we were ten minutes ago!"'

One year the Frasers even went to the Birdsville Races—along with half of Melbourne and Sydney suburbia. 'We counted 257 light aircraft,' said Tam. 'They had all landed on the Birdsville airstrip at roughly the same time—with no air traffic control whatsoever. It was like a giant swarm of bees! By ten o'clock in the morning there was already a pile of empty beer cans three feet high outside the Birdsville pub.

'As we were standing around a young chap got on his motorbike and started to zoom off with far too many revs, flipped, and landed in the dust, much to the onlookers' enjoyment. Then off we went to the actual races. There was lots of betting and lots more drinking and most of the spectators were pretty surprised to see their Prime Minister there. At one stage some chaps came up to me with huge grins on their faces and offered me a can, saying: "Like a beer, Tamie?" Oh, thanks! I said, and I took it. But something in their smiles warned me and as I ripped open the tab I pointed the can the other way, and to their astonishment, *they* were the ones who were showered in white froth!

'We loved our stay in Birdsville, but I felt the people who had come seemed to be searching for something which they obviously couldn't find back in the suburbs—perhaps the camaraderie and recognition of each person's identity in his or her own right which you find only in the country. In Birdsville everyone wanted to be friends with everyone, they wanted to know each other, they wanted to be happy and say good morning to each other because they never did at home.

The sad part was that it took 27 tons of beer to give them the courage.'

But the big cities of course are where most Australians live. In Melbourne Tamie opened a pie factory, in Hobart an art exhibition, and in Darwin a crocodile farm. In Sydney she launched a book, in Alice Springs an appeal and in Cairns a patrol boat. 'I made a point of covering as great a cross-section of enterprises and life-styles as possible,' she said. One day she even conducted an orchestra. 'Malcolm and I attended the International Press Dinner which Australia hosted in the Great Hall of the Melbourne Art Gallery. John Hopkins conducted the youth orchestra in a marvellous rendition of Waltzing Matilda, and everyone cheered and wanted them to play it again because they were all so delighted with it.

'After dinner Malcolm and I went over to congratulate the orchestra on playing it so well and John Hopkins said, "Come on, Prime Minister, we'll play it again—and this time you conduct!" Malcolm looked at me in horror, in absolute wild-eyed horror, and said, "Oh no—Tam will do it!"

'So I got up there full of fight. I grabbed the baton and started swooshing my arms around in the air and I had on a coat with big draped, sort of droopy sleeves and I must have looked from behind, like Mary Poppins about to take off. Anyway the orchestra came in, but just behind the beat. Now I was aware from watching at concerts that a conductor always keeps slightly ahead of the beat in order to lead the orchestra, but I simply couldn't do that.

'I was beating in time to the music and so they kept falling a split second behind me and thus we got gradually slower and *slower*.

'It was desperate—just like a battery running flat! I looked at John Hopkins in panic and he gestured frantically for me to speed up. So I waved my arms faster and faster, not listening to the music at all, but just keeping my arms flying in time to the rhythm in my head. The orchestra followed and we positively romped home through the last few bars, ending up with a rousing cheer from the astonished audience!'

Tam went to Adelaide many times as well. Caroline Sande (who took over as her secretary in February, 1980, when Amanda Derham moved to Melbourne) told me about Tam going shopping in Adelaide one day in a spare hour between official engagements. As she was trying on a pair of shoes in a city department store a woman came up to her and said:

'Excuse me, dear, but has anyone told you that you look just like Tamie Fraser?'

'I am,' said Tam.

'Yes, you are,' said the woman. 'Just like her.'

'Yes, I am!'

'I agree. It's quite remarkable. The spitting-image of Tamie Fraser!'

'*But I am Tamie Fraser!*'

'Ooh.'

Included on Tam's map was a section of Papua-New Guinea, also dotted with bright pins. 'Malcolm and I went there in February, 1977,' she told me. 'We flew to Port Moresby then on to Lae, Wewak, Vanimo, Mount Hagen, Mendi and Daru—all in the space of four days. We were the first official visitors from Australia the Papua-New Guineans had had since they gained their independence.

'One night in Port Moresby we were treated to a proper New Guinea feast, with pork and chicken cooked in the ground and yams and sweet potatoes— it was all quite delicious. The evening was warm and still and we sat outside on chairs and some islanders came on all dressed up in beads and grasses and shells, and they danced for us. I wish I had some photographs of the dancing! I was sitting next to Michael Somare who was shrieking with laughter and enjoying the whole thing hugely and hoping we were too—and we were! But it was certainly different to anything we'd seen before!'

I pressed Tam for details. 'Well, it's rather difficult for *me* to describe,' she replied, and when she showed me the program, I understood why:

CONTEMPORARY TROBRIAND ISLANDS
CRICKET CHANTS
THREE PIECES:
Prepared and presented by the Gala Tona Club.
1 TAPIOKWA: This chant is supposed to represent
   the masturbation of the male organ.
2 GALA TONA: The words literally mean 'not much'
   but figuratively means the man having an erection
   readily.
3 MWEKI: The Trobriand Society is permissive as far
   as sex goes. The actions represent the sexual inter-
   course motions.

This was Tam's second visit to Papua-New Guinea.
She had been once before in 1975 when Malcolm was
Leader of the Opposition. 'We went with the
Whitlams to celebrate Strine-Pissin'-Off-Day,' she said.
'*What?*'
'That's pidgin for Independence Day! Prince Charles
was there representing the Queen. He arrived in a
Mixmaster-Belonga-God, in other words a helicopter.
He was referred to as the Piccaninny-Bilonga-Mrs.
Queen! And you know his official Prince of Wales
insignia with the three ostrich plumes? That was called
Grass-Bilonga-Arse-Bilonga-Chicken! But apparently
the Prince entered into the spirit of the occasion won-
derfully, and when the time came for him to leave
Papua-New Guinea, he declared: "Me all bugger-off-
finish!"'
   And so when the time came for me to leave Nareen,
how could I not declare "me all bugger-off-finish!"
as well?

Chapter 19
CHOGM —
MELBOURNE

The Prime Minister of Australia rose to his feet before the lectern. The Heads of Government of 41 Commonwealth nations looked up to give him their attention. The audience packed in to the Melbourne Town Hall grew silent and still. Malcolm drew a short breath to begin . . . and at that precise moment the town hall organist George Truman launched into a spirited rendition of 'La Ci Darem La Mano' (You'll lay your hand in mine, dear) from Mozart's 'Don Giovanni'.

Sitting at the back of the Hall, Eda and I couldn't help but join in the general laughter and gentle applause which ensued. The Prime Minister raised his hands in defeat to Mozart, and smiled, that wonderful rare smile of his which softens his features and lights up his whole face. The organist, sensing something amiss, positively romped through the last few bars of the music. Then the Prime Minister, still smiling, approached the lectern once more and began his address.

Curiously enough, this was not an inauspicious start to the Commonwealth Heads of Government Conference held in Melbourne in October 1981. Delegates and audience alike had visibly relaxed. The atmosphere had melted to one of warmth and goodwill. And, as I remarked to Tam later that evening, an injection of the human element into a program of otherwise clockwork precision was not such an inappropriate reminder to a group of people in whose hands rest the welfare of a quarter of the world's population.

The Heads of Government were an impressive sight as they sat around their big semi-circular table on the dais of the Melbourne Town Hall in strict alphabetical order. Behind them stood the flag of each nation. Before them in the centre of the circle lay a giant CHOGM symbol, surrounded by a carpet of flowers in, at Tamie's insistence, the Australian national colours—green, gold and white.

We were already seated when the HOGs had arrived about 15 minutes beforehand to allow for press photographs to be taken before the Opening ceremony began. This was the first occasion on which they had met together in Melbourne, and probably many of them had not seen each other since the last CHOGM in Lusaka in 1979. I watched with interest as their greetings ranged from a half-hearted wave across the stage to a prolonged handshake or even a ponderous embrace.

While they stood around and the flashlights blazed, Eda and I played Pick the PM, and then I was struck by how much in real life people look like their photographs, absurd thought. Pierre Trudeau was chatting to Lee Kwan Yew, his hand in his pocket, super cool. Margaret Thatcher, impeccable all in black, seemed pensive and detached. Mrs. Ghandi was much smaller than I had imagined, a diminutive figure as she stood there in her sari, only her face revealing the steel needed to hold power in the world's largest democracy. Prince Mabandla, PM of Swaziland, looked a splendid figure in gown and feathers, and amongst the others there was a colourful sprinkling of turbans, kaftans, saris and gold-braided military uniforms. Mr. Muldoon of New Zealand, I noted with a smile, wore a suit, tie and expression of dark grey.

Outside the Town Hall, thousands of people had lined Swanston Street to watch the Heads of Government arrive. They had clapped and cheered as each walked up the red carpet into the Hall while the Australian Naval Band from HMAS Cerberus played appropriate music: 'Rock Around the Clock' for the Commonwealth Secretary-General, Mr. Shridath Ramphal, 'Swinging Safari' for Malcolm, and for Mrs. Thatcher—the theme from 'Superman'.

In his opening address Malcolm urged Commonwealth leaders to send the rest of the world a 'clear message of concern and commitment' on north-south issues. He said that the message was as important as the practical steps the conference might take on food, energy and trade. 'I am convinced,' he said, 'that our generation of leaders will ultimately be judged largely in terms of their success or failure in reconciling the interests of the rich and poor countries of the Earth. For if they are not reconciled, the world in which we shall live out our lives and which our children shall inherit, will be an unhappy one, condemned to turmoil and bitterness. Those who fail to recognise the gravity and drama of the issues disguised by the rather bland term "North-South dialogue" are guilty of a serious failure of historical imagination.'

While giving the north-south issue top priority, Australia's PM also moved to contain divisions within the Commonwealth over Namibia, and the Gleneagles Agreement—issues which his long time adversary, Mr. Muldoon, had been stirring the previous day. Malcolm told his audience that southern African issues were 'very complex, and inevitably there will be some differences between us. But we all abhor apartheid, regard it as both inhumane and politically suicidal, and want to see it abolished.'

The address was well received. Mr. Ramphal spoke next, followed by the New Boy of the Commonwealth, Robert Mugabe of Zimbabwe. Then came Mrs. Thatcher, Ratu Sir Kamisese Mara of Fiji and Mrs. Ghandi, finishing with a dynamic and witty address from Comrade Forbes Burnham, President of Guyana. Tamie, all in peach, sat in the front row with the other CHOGM spouses—and beamed. The conference was away to a flying start.

'It was quite an operation,' Tam told me later, when it was all over. 'The planning for CHOGM began about a year before. The Exhibition Building was chosen for the actual Conference because it has such an enormous floor space, and the first problem was to make this huge barn-like structure and its modern annexes functional and pleasant to work in. The architects divided it up very cleverly. First there was the actual meeting chamber, then there was a relaxation area for the delegates, sub-committee rooms, private offices for each delegation, a 23 hour-a-day telex service, a separate area including three television studios for the 400 foreign press representatives coming to cover the Conference, a bank, some bars, a news agency, gift shops—it was a huge undertaking.

'Malcolm was shown samples of suggested colours for the temporary walls, the carpet, the curtains, the furniture, &c. and he took one look at them and said, "Tam will do all that." So the people in charge came along to me, and I've not had much experience at furnishing those sorts of areas but I could tell at a glance the carpets chosen were the wrongs tonings to go with the walls, which didn't match the chairs and or/the curtains. The fawns were all different, the mustards didn't match, there was bright blue and orange in one room, and something else clashing in another. Anyway we looked at endless samples and got that straightened out.

'Next there was a program to be planned for the wives. It wasn't meant to be mandatory, just something pleasant to do each day if they wished. Then we arranged a big dinner to be held at the Hilton on the third night of the Conference. Our concept for that dinner was to have people from the business community, the Church, aboriginal groups, ethnic communities, the unions, the law, farming—representatives from as wide a spectrum of Australian society as possible. We tried out the food beforehand, the menu that we'd chosen, and decided the sweet wasn't as we'd hoped so we changed that. We arranged for the flowers, their colour scheme and where they were to be placed; background music, where the musicians would sit and how loudly they should play; the seating plan, to ensure compatible tables—the planning was punctilious. We wanted to do the very best we could.'

The Heads of Government had been arriving in Melbourne on and off for two days before the opening. They were met at the airport by Ministers or senior members of parliament and taken to their hotels. Then they came in groups to pay a formal call on the Prime Minister of Australia in his suite at the Hilton. One morning 15 Heads of Government called on Malcolm consecutively, while Tamie sat in a little room next door and received the wives. They had a cup of tea or coffee with each—and Tam said Malcolm's capacity proved far greater than hers!

The Queen, also in Melbourne for the event (although playing no official role in the Conference itself), on the night of the Opening gave a banquet for the Heads of Government aboard the royal yacht Brittania, docked at Station Pier. The day before she had paid a surprise visit to the Exhibition Building to inspect the facilities set up for the Conference. Derek Ingram, an English editor who had covered every CHOGM since they started in 1971, described those facilities as the best he had yet seen.

Next morning, Thursday October 1, the Conference began. The HOGs sped from their hotels to the Exhibition Buildings in convoys under heavy police escort, choppers hovered overhead, and on street corners closed-circuit television cameras kept watch, while all around the city nearly 4000 police, security guards and troops carried out the biggest security exercise in Australia's history.

Meanwhile, Tam was coping with the wives. 'There were about 30 wives of Commonwealth Heads or Ministers to look after, and although some of them, like Mrs. Lee and Adi Lady Lala Mara were old friends from previous CHOGMs, many of them I'd never met before. So I had to memorise faces and names and the pronunciation of those names, as well as something about them and the countries they came from. I had asked for photographs and tried to do my homework before they arrived, because it was my job to introduce all the wives, both to each other and to everyone else, and generally look after them—if someone was standing aside and looking a bit shy, make sure they were included in the group—you know the sort of thing.'

Caroline Sande, Tam's Secretary, was always on hand to help, an invaluable support.

On Thursday, after a conducted tour of the National Gallery, the wives were given a luncheon at Ripponlea, a National Trust mansion in Elsternwick, Victorian in style, with a lovely garden. Eda and I were there amongst the 100 or so guests waiting to meet them. At the luncheon I found myself seated next to Mrs. Sally Mugabe on one side, and the wife of a diplomat from Mauritius, whose name I can't remember—call her Mme. French—on the other. After drinks we settled down at our tables and I turned to Mme. French, and said: 'Is this your first visit to Melbourne?'

'You really must come to Mauritius,' she replied. 'It ees very beautiful.'

'Oh, yes, I'd love to,' I said. 'What part of Mauritius are you from?'

'It ees very beautiful in Mauritius. You really must come.'

'Yes, I'm sure it is!' I said. 'Do you live in the capital?'

'You really must come to Mauritius. It ees very beautiful,' she said.

As a plate of steaming asparagus was placed before us, I remembered Tam telling me that if I was struggling with conversation, to ask about children. Women all around the world love talking about their children. Children are a great common bond. 'Tell me,' I said to Mme. French, fighting down the urge to speak louder, 'do you have any children?'

'You really must come to Mauritius! It ees very beautiful!' she said. With a sinking feeling I turned to Sally Mugabe, seated on my left. 'Mrs. Mugabe, do you have any children?'

'Yes,' she replied, 'but they both died while Robert was in prison.' I wish I was back at Balmoral, I thought.

But Sally Mugabe, obviously (achingly) used to coping with the question, calmly went on to explain to me how she now devoted her time to improving the position of women in Zimbabwe. She described some of the problems faced by women there, both black and white, and I found her a fascinating and charming companion.

When the guests had finished their chicken with almond and cherry sauce, and orange sorbet, Tamie announced there would be a fashion parade. To a jazzy musical accompaniment, 12 models displayed the work of some of Australia's top designers. There was Adele Palmer DBA featuring 'relaxed exuberant volume'. From Zampatti, ' . . . the line, lean and languid.' Covers presented 'texture, line, dash,' and Simona displayed clothes 'uncomplicated, yet with undeniable impact'. The reaction by the CHOGM wives was uncomplicated, but with undeniable impact as well. They loved it.

'Which designs did you like best?' I asked my friend on my right.

'You really must come to Mauritius. It ees very beautiful,' she said.

There was one spouse, however, conspicuously absent from the fashion parade at Ripponlea. Mr. Denis Thatcher spent the day visiting the Loy Yang and Hazelwood power plants in the LaTrobe Valley.

Another day Tam took the wives to the Melbourne Zoo. They fed the pelicans and cuddled the koalas and patted the kangaroos, but undoubtedly the highlight of the visit, according to my mother who went along that day to help, was the giraffes. 'Several of the wives had never seen a giraffe before,' Mum told me, 'and so we found the giraffe enclosure and peered in through the wire and ooohhed and aaahhed.

'Giraffes are apparently gloriously free of any inhibitions and while we were standing there a blushing young female giraffe was approached by a dashing young male, and, my dear, right in front of our eyes nature proceeded to take it course. As you can imagine with such enormous animals, it wasn't a spectacle one could possibly pretend to ignore. Seismographs must have been recording it all over the state. The result was that half the CHOGM wives took one look and hurried off down the path, scarlet with embarassment, while the other half remained glued to the wire, determined not to miss a single passionate moment. And yes!' said Mum, laughing. 'Before you even ask—I was definitely one of the latter!'

After the Sydney bombing at CHOGRM, 1979, security was a constant strain. The wives were protected by plain-clothes policewomen wherever they went. The HOGs never moved without an armed escort. The city bristled with police. Tamie told me that as each night went by she and Malcolm used to crawl into bed saying well, that's another day gone—and they're all still alive! Bombs were a major worry and metal scanners like those at airports were used at many functions. I remember one distinguished guest giving everyone a terrible turn one day when he set the alarm bells shrieking with his metal knees, implanted by surgery some years before.

While the HOGs debated the problems of apartheid in South Africa, Tam took her charges to the Botanical Gardens. 'We were met by Dr. Churchill, the director of the gardens, and Mrs. Churchill, and there were guides as well to show us around. We set off down the path and hadn't gone very far at all when Dr Churchill said: "Now this plant you might know. It is a strelitzia, a native of South Africa." Oh dear, I thought. "And what's this plant right down here?" I asked him, and hurried my charges on to less politically contentious species!

'When we had completed our tour of the Gardens, which all the wives enjoyed very much, Mrs. Churchill presented them each a little lavender bag, organza with lace around the edge, and made quite on her own initiative with the lavender from the botanical gardens. The visitors were delighted—and it was one of the many small gestures which kept appearing throughout CHOGM in Melbourne. Melbourne really put its best foot forward for CHOGM. There was a widespread feeling that we were the window for Australia, and people rallied around and tried to do their best. This was very warming to us and showed that we had a depth of support which was not being reflected in the press.'

Many of the CHOGM leaders commented to Malcolm on the press coverage of the Conference. They said that in reports all the emphasis had been on side issues or personality problems and that the main issues had hardly been addressed. 'Some of the Africans remarked to me that if this was an example of a free press, then they didn't want a bar of it!' Malcolm told me. 'They said they thought freedom meant responsibility.'

The press issue which sparked the greatest ire however was a rumour about Malcolm's health which surfaced a few days after the Conference began. A Sydney newspaper reported that the Prime Minister had been seen visiting the Peter McCallum cancer clinic in Melbourne where he had had some tissue removed for testing. He would resign in four weeks' time because of bad health, the report said. The story was immediately denied by the PM and his staff, but it continued to boil. 'I was so busy rushing around looking after the wives that I didn't hear about it until we got to Canberra to the HOG's weekend retreat,' Tam said. 'I was driving in from the airport in Canberra and my driver, said, "They're being a bit hard on the Boss, aren't they, Mrs. F?" And I said, what do you mean? And he said,"You know, this cancer thing," and I said I have not the faintest idea what you're talking about. And when I reached The Lodge Caroline Sande, my secretary, said Nationwide has rung and asked you to go on television tonight about the PM's health. And I said, it's a complete fabrication! I'm not going on any television program! I've got 80 people to dinner!

'Then Phoebe rang up from school in floods of tears, and said, "Mum, I've just seen Dad on television! Has he or hasn't he got cancer? I must know! Please, tell me!" she said, sobbing into the telephone.

'I was so angry! That a made-up, easily-checkable story was hurting my children to this extent—and I knew the rest of the family would be worried sick as well—it made me furious! So I rang Caroline and said, tell Nationwide I've changed my mind. Before I go out to dinner tonight, I will come on their program.

'When I arrived at Nationwide I tried to cool down a bit, but it obviously wasn't very successful because young Hugh was out watching the program with some friends and one of them told me later that when he saw me walk on, before I'd even opened my mouth, he said: "She's wild! Oh boy, look at Mum! She's really wild!"'

'I've only come here tonight because I am absolutely outraged at the reports!' Tam said to Richard Carleton when the cameras rolled. She stressed how easily the facts could have been checked, how upset her children had been—and asked how would Malcolm have had time this week to go to a clinic anyway? 'Malcolm is very well,' she finished up, 'and as you can see has been continuing on this week with CHOGM.'

'Well,' said Richard Carleton, giving her that bland, mocking smile of his, and completely disregarding everything she had said, 'how is your husband's health?'

It was too much. 'I've said he's fit!' Tam snapped. 'How often do I have to repeat myself?' Then with great dignity she rose to her feet and said, 'Well, thank you very much. I think I'll go off to my dinner.' And walked out. It caused a sensation.

'A grand exit in the heroic mould!' said The Sun. 'Undoubtedly the most marvellous piece of theatre on television last week!' said the Sydney Morning Herald. The ABC switchboard was jammed with calls over the incident and Tam received literally hundreds of letters of support. The next night at dinner at The Lodge Mrs. Thatcher commented loudly and within easy hearing of the press how well the Prime Minister looked, and added: 'you'll outlast the lot of them—including the journalists!'

But she was too far busy entertaining the HOGs to give the matter another thought. During their 're-

'treat' weekend the visitors were taken to the National Capital Development Commission exhibition at Regatta Point and shown a film of Canberra as it was twenty years ago—and many expressed great surprise at the development of the city. Another highlight of their program was lunch at Huntly, the beautiful property of Mr. John Gale just out of Canberra.

Back in Melbourne Mrs. Thatcher called on the Conference to endorse the United Nations 'contact group' in its present efforts to negotiate with South Africa and the frontline states over Namibian independence. Mr. Muldoon, Malcolm's bete noire, was again causing trouble. He had been a thorn in Malcolm's side at CHOGM Gleneagles, at CHOGM Lusaka and also at CHOGM in Sydney. Now in Melbourne in 1981 he was stirring the pot again. He had already caused problems over Namibia and the Gleneagles agreement, and now, referring to Robert Mugabe's criticism of the New Zealand government's attitude to the Springbok tour, Mr. Muldoon had said: 'Well, I suppose when you've been in the jungle shooting people it is a bit difficult to understand!' Mr. Mugabe was outraged. Malcolm was furious.

On the last day of talks Tamie took the wives to the country to visit Cruden Farm, home of Dame Elisabeth Murdoch, near Langwarrin. At tables covered in flowers under a large white marquee 108 guests dined on rock lobster and noisettes of spring lamb before enjoying a wander through the Cruden Farm's beautiful garden.

The main achievement of the 1981 Commonwealth Heads of Government Conference was the Melbourne Declaration, a statement setting out 16 points of agreement on how rich and poor countries could unite to combat third world poverty. Mr. Muldoon dismissed it as 'pious platitudes'. But as Mrs. Ghandi commented, 'Busy men and women accustomed to count every minute of their time would not spend a week together were they not convinced of the value of this meeting to promote the common good.'

'And when it was all over,' said Tam, 'when all the

visitors had flown back to their own countries, we
had two big parties at the Exhibition Building and I
think there were 1000 people at each. Everyone who
had worked to make it a success—car drivers, police,
telephone maintenance men, electricians, plumbers,
cleaners, carpetlayers, caterers, office staff—anyone
who had anything to do with the set-up of CHOGM
we asked back to the Exhibition Building before it was
dismantled. Malcolm and I went to each party, and
we all had a wonderful post mortem, recounting all
the things we'd seen and done.' There was plenty to
tell. This had been the largest international conference
ever staged in Australia, and with meetings held only
bi-annually, it will probably be a very long time before
CHOGM visits Australia again.

To be honest, it will probably be a very long time
before I visit Mauritius as well.

Chapter 20
CHILDREN

In the winter of 1980 when Mark and Angela Fraser accompanied their parents on a tour of Western Australia, Peter Costigan wrote in the Melbourne 'Herald': 'Most people were surprised to meet the Fraser children and many indicated they had not known there were any.

'Since Mr. Fraser became Prime Minister, the Frasers deliberately have kept their children out of the limelight. Mrs. Fraser in particular is known to believe that while they were growing up their privacy had to be protected. But they emerged in public over the last week with considerable style and learnt a lot about how the Prime Minister operates on tour.'

In the article Mark was described as 'tall like his father, and affable.' On reading this, Malcolm remarked wistfully: 'Why couldn't it say "tall and affable like his father?"'.

This was actually Angela's second experience of public life. Two years earlier when Tam had been unable to attend a gala dinner held in Darwin to celebrate the Northern Territory's recent self-government, the PM had asked his elder daughter to accompany him instead.

'I'd never shaken 300 hands before!' she told me on her return. 'Dad and I stood in the receiving line in the ballroom at the Park Royal Motel in Darwin and greeted the guests as they arrived. Then we went downstairs to meet the Governor General and Ladv Cowen. A big crowd had gathered outside the entrance to the hotel, all jostling each other and shouting abuse at Dad. I found it rather daunting but I stood there trying to look composed and thinking all the time, "Is this what Mum has to put up with?" But soon the GG arrived and I managed my courtesy without tripping over my long dress and then we all made our way upstairs for the dinner.'

Angela was seated next to Sir Zelman Cowen at the official table. 'He was charming and made such an effort to put me at ease. Our table was raised on a dais and as I looked out over the room I noticed a waitress with red hair and a white blouse which didn't quite reach to the top of her tight black skirt serving wine to the guests. And every now and then as she did so she had a quick swig from the bottle. I couldn't believe my eyes! Then she came over to our table, stepped on to the dais to refill our glasses, and in ringing tones started chatting up Dad and Lady Cowen. Lady Cowen said to her: "Tell me, what do you do?" "Well," she said, one hand on her hip, the other swinging the wine bottle by its neck from side to side: "I'm studying brain surgery at Darwin University, but on weekends *I sell me body*!" Lady Cowen's face was a real picture!' said Angela.

'The waitress came back to our table a bit later on in the evening, again with bottle in hand. "Wanna 'nother drink, eh, Mal?" she said. "Thanks," said Dad. "Mind if I join you?" she said. "Oh, please do," said Dad, looking a bit non-plussed but pushing one of his glasses over towards her. But not a bit of it. It was up with the bottle and glug glug glug! But then the security guys noticed what was happening and came over and hustled her away.'

How much do children suffer when their parents hold high public office? How does the publicity and the pressure—and the inevitable separations—affect their lives? In my capacity as fond aunt I have watched the Fraser children growing up over the years, held their hands and their heads, wiped their noses and eyes. But it was not until quite recently that I sat them down and asked them what it had been like to have a father the PM.

'Well, to me Dad was always just Dad,' said Phoebe. "I was only nine when he became Prime Minister and I really didn't understand that there was anything different about him from other people's dads until late one night at school when we were chatting in the dormitory, after lights out, about what we'd been doing in the holidays. I was regaling everyone with how my two big brothers were better shots than Dad's security guards. We'd been out on a picnic in the paddocks at Nareen and Mark and Hugh had pinned a target to a gum tree and had beaten the security guys in a shooting competition. And someone said: "Gawd! Who's your father?" And I said he's Malcolm Fraser. And she said: "Gawd, why does he have security guards?" and I said in case someone tries to stop him doing his job—doesn't yours? I mean, that was about as far as my understanding went and it wasn't until that moment that I realised that my father's job was somehow special and that my life outside the family may become different because of that.'

'Inside the family it made no difference. Dad was still Dad. He'd always been in the papers and he'd always been busy. We were either away at boarding school or with Mum at Nareen for the hols and Dad came to see us as much as he could. Mum always managed to be with us for anything important in between. For instance, I remember my school sports were held right in the middle of the Commonwealth Games.

I told her *not* to come, but she flew down from Brisbane at lunchtime, watched me running in the hurdles then flew back in time to be with Dad for the presentation of medals that night. And if both of them had to be away then Grannie and Grandfather were In Charge. Grannie was my second mother. I got on with her tremendously! We'd talk for hours and giggle over all the same things. Grandfather was different. He didn't like to waste words and just chat. But that was special too. And if they were away then there was always Arna Fraser, you or Eda or Uncle Hugh. We were never on our own.'

But security was an ever-present problem and I wondered how much that impinged upon the children's lives. 'In 1975 over the election and everything I had to have security guards with me at school. Mum says I hated it, but I don't really remember. I think when you're young you have a knack for blocking out horrible things. But later on, when I was in second or third form at Melbourne Grammar, there had been numerous death threats against us kids and apparently there were security people on duty outside the school, but I wasn't told.

'One afternoon the teacher on duty asked me was I going to aths. training at Olympic Park that evening? I said oh, I don't think so, and then later on I said well, maybe I might, and then oh, no, probably not.

'I changed my mind at least four times in an hour, having talked to different friends—were they going or not—and the teacher was getting furious with me! And I couldn't understand why it made any difference, why I had to make a decision, because none of the other kids were being asked their plans. But apparently if I was going to go to Olympic Park the teacher had to arrange security guys to go with me—and she was trying to protect me from knowing about it!'

In January 1976 Mark started work as a jackaroo on a station in the Riverina district of NSW. 'Dad drove me all the way up to Deniliquin from Nareen in an old Holden ute (I was still too young for a Victorian licence). He settled me in to my new job, then hopped in a plane and flew off to Canberra to get settled in to his!'

In the Riverina Mark was protected as far as possible from undue publicity by the people he worked with and by the local community, who thought that any young fella had the right to live his own life and should be left alone to get on with it. But when a reporter came along he was never told—Get Lost! Mark doesn't want to see you! Instead, in the polite but unmoveable way of country people, he was told: "I think he's out on the tractor somewhere," or "I'm afraid he's getting a mob of sheep from the back paddock," or "he was around this morning but I don't see him now—perhaps he's gone into town?"' One day when Mark was driving into Deniliquin he came across a car parked by the side of the road, obviously broken down. He pulled up beside it and asked if he could help. The driver, puce in the face and covered with dust, said could he have a lift back to the nearest point of civilisation? 'Sure,' said Mark. 'Hop in.'

As they drove along Mark chatted away to his passenger about local matters and when they reached town dropped him of at the local garage, and went his way. 'That's a great young fella,' said the passenger to the garage-owner, as he watched Mark drive away.

'That's Mark Fraser, the Prime Minister's son,' said the garage-owner.

'*What?*'

'Yes, that's him alright. But what's the problem?'

'I'm a reporter,' the man groaned, 'and I've been sent up here especially to write a story about Mark Fraser. I've been trying to track him down for three days!'

Sometimes, however, the reverse occurred. One day Mark was driving through a small town in outback NSW and decided to stop for a beer at the local pub. 'There was a group of young blokes standing around the bar discussing employment and what jobs their old men did for a living,' Mark told me. 'I ordered a beer and the bloke behind the counter said to me: "What does your old man do?" I mumbled, well, he tries to run the country. "Oh yeah? And mine's a bookie on Mars!" said the barman. I just let it go and talked about something else.

'But a few minutes later he came up to me again, and said: "Your old man—he doesn't really run the country, does he?" And I said yeah. "Can you prove it?" and I thought, bloody hell—you know? I knew the family was home at Nareen at the time, so I got on the 'phone and asked to speak to Dad. As Dad came on the line the barman grabbed the 'phone. Now Dad's voice is very distinctive and all he said was: "Hullo?" "Jesus Christ!" the barman said. "*It is you!*" "No," said Dad, "it's me. What do you want?" "Oh nothing! Sorry to have bothered you, sir!" the barman said, and hung up—and I didn't have to pay for another drink the rest of the night!'

Hugh told me of another Identity Crisis, as he called it, which happened to him when he was staying at The Lodge and was dressed in a dinner jacket ready to go out to his first formal dance. 'I was still too young to drive so I rang for a taxi,' said Hugh. 'The girl asked me what name? And I said, Fraser. "Address?" The Lodge. "Okay," she said. "It'll be there in five minutes." Well, I waited for ages but there was no sign of the taxi, so I rang again. "It's on it's way," the girl assured me. "Should be there any minute!" So I waited some more and still no taxi came and by this time I was running awfully late for my party. So mum got on the phone in high dudgeon, and said "This is Tamara Fraser speaking! *Where is my son's taxi?*" and they were frightfully apologetic—they'd thought the call was just a hoax!'

'There were some pretty nasty kidnapping threats against all of us at various times,' Angela said. 'When I was living in Melbourne and studying interior design at the RMIT, I was out at the movies one night with a friend. We were watching "Close Encounters of the Third Kind" and about halfway through a notice suddenly flashed across the bottom of the screen, saying: *Will* (the name of the guy I was with) *please report to the Manager's office at once.*

'We thought, "My God, what's happened, have his parents had a terrible car accident? Has someone dropped dead?" You can imagine how we felt. He went straight out then returned a few minutes later, and whispered "We've got to go." So I followed him out with my heart thumping and as we were walking up the steps he told me there'd been a kidnapping threat and he had to take me home.

'After all the things I'd been imagining this seemed

almost a relief! The police were outside the theatre waiting for me. There were State police and Federal police involved and I think it was the Feds who drove me back to my flat. Two State policemen were waiting there with Gina, my flatmate. They had taken their pistols off and lain them on the coffee table. Anyway eventually they all dispersed, except for one guy who slept on the sofa and stayed all night. I had to have someone following me around to classes for a few days after that.'

When Angela first left school she had spent a year reading arts at the Australian National University in Canberra living with her parents at The Lodge. '"Fraser" is not an unusual name and I keep pretty quiet and it didn't occur to anybody that I might be the PM's daughter,' said Angela. 'We went away on a uni camping excursion not long after the start of term. There were 30 of us and we all slept jammed into three big tents. The last night as we were going to bed someone said: "Fraser's a bastard!" and a fierce political argument broke out with everyone competing to see who could say the vilest thing about Dad. I took it in silence for awhile then I mumbled something about how stuffy it was in the tent, gathered up my things and slept the rest of the night on the ground outside.

'When we returned next day the bus drove around Canberra dropping people off at their homes because we all had so much heavy luggage and camping gear, but I could hardly remain anonymous and be dropped off at The Lodge! So I said just drop me off on the other side of the park. They said "course not, we'll take you home—it's no trouble". But I said, thank you, but I enjoy a brisk walk! So they left me standing on the side of the road not far from Adelaide Avenue and probably thought I didn't have a home at all!'

Later on that year while Tam and Malcolm were overseas Angela spent six weeks boarding in one of the university colleges. 'By this time I guess the word had got around,' said Angela, 'and one of my friends told me that some kids had come up to her at the end of my stay there and said in absolute amazement: "But she's not too bad! She's really quite nice!"'

During the '77 election campaign there was a cartoon in one of the papers which featured a whale holding up a banner on which was written: *Vote 1 Phoebe Fraser, December 10!*

'Phoebe, did you really save the whales?' I asked.

'No! It was all a big beatup!' Phoebe laughed. 'I was in 6th grade at boarding school at the time and for some reason I became interested in whales and I asked Dad about them, didn't he think they should stop being shot? The issue was topical at the time and when Dad was next questioned about it by someone he said, oh yes, Phoebe's been tackling me about the whales—and the press picked it up and ran. It was blown out of all proportion.'

Over the years Malcolm had some tough things said about him in the press and I asked Phoebe how that had affected her. 'Well, at the age of nine you don't read the papers,' she said, 'and when I was old enough to read them, I was also old enough to take what they said with a grain of salt.'

'What about when the papers kept saying how badly he was doing in the polls, how unpopular his government was—how no-one liked him?'

'Well, we knew that at the same time he was working his guts out trying to do his best for the country.'

'But how did you feel when there were headlines accusing him of breaking promises, telling lies?'

'Look, Pete!' she said, bridling at last at my line of questioning. 'It wasn't easy. It was bloody hell sometimes. But Dad never ever broke a promise to us. He never ever lied to us. Dad was Dad, and we knew what he was *really* like. So whatever the world happened to think of him never made the slightest bit of difference.'

I couldn't think of another thing to say.

Chapter 21
COLLECTED LETTERS

The mail Tamie received at The Lodge was constant and amazingly diverse, Caroline Sande told me. 'On one occasion after she had made an appearance on Sydney television, Mrs. Fraser received a letter congratulating her on her performance and another critisising it—both posted from the same letter box on the same day!' And strangely enough there were more letters over a full moon.

'One old lady used to write two or three times a week.' Caroline said. 'She was obviously very lonely. She said she was confined to an old people's home, and surrounded by Labor voters. We used to save her letters up and answer them every so often in a batch.'

Some idea of the range of problems Tam was asked to tackle can be gained from this random selection of her replies:

Dear Mrs . . .

Thank you very much for your letter about your pensions.

Regarding your telephone bill, it is possible for you as pensioners to obtain a one-third reduction from your annual telephone rental, by applying to your local Telecom office — if you have not already done so.

However, I shall certainly speak to Malcolm about your problems, and if you have any other worries, please let me know.

Yours sincerely, etc.
(Mrs. Malcolm Fraser)

Dear Mrs . . .

I agree with you that sometimes the Speaker appears to romp through the Lord's Prayer. I have spoken to the Prime Minister on your behalf about it.

Yours sincerely, etc

Dear Mrs . . .

It would indeed be good if your parents could be with you here in Australia.

I am contacting the Minister for Immigration and Ethnic Affairs, Mr. MacKellar, who is a sympathetic and understanding man. He will be able to tell you what the situation is.

Thank you for your letter, and please send my regards to your parents.

Yours sincerely, etc.

Dear Mrs . . .

The Prime Minister first said 'Life wasn't meant to be easy' in a lecture he gave in 1971, and I have attached the whole paragraph for you so that you can settle your bet!

With best wishes,
Yours sincerely, etc.

(ENCLOSED: EXTRACT FROM THE 1971 ALFRED DEAKIN LECTURE: 'Towards 2000 Challenge to Australia'

'Arnold Toynbee once wrote twelve volumes to demonstrate and analyse the cause of the rise and fall of nations. His thesis can be condensed to a sentence, and is simply stated: That through history nations are confronted by a series of challenges and whether they survive or whether they fall to the wayside, depends on the manner and character of their response. Simple, and perhaps one of the few things that is self-evident. It involves a conclusion about the past that life has not been easy for people or for nations, and an assumption for the future that the condition will not alter. There is within me some part of the metaphysic, and thus I would add that life is not meant to be easy.'

Dear Mr. and Mrs. . . .

Thank you very much for your concerned note about the harp seals.

I have had many letters like yours drawing attention to the problem, and I have passed them on to the Minister concerned. It does seem a cruel way of treating such rare animals, and I think it is wonderful that so many people throughout the world share your concern.

With best wishes,
Yours sincerely, etc.

Dear Mrs . . .

Thank you very much for your letter about the export of horses.

The incident you mentioned was a most regrettable one, and it does seem such a cruel way of treating such noble animals at the end of their lives. The Government has however decided that it should have greater control over the conditions under which animals are to be exported, and live horses for export have now been included in the Third Schedule of the Customs (Prohibited Exports) Regulations, which means that they can now only be exported under specific conditions, and with the approval of a Commonwealth officer authorised by the Minister for Primary Industry. These new measures will give the Commonwealth the necessary power to ensure far greater supervision over their shipment.

Yours sincerely, etc.

Dear Mrs . . .

I received your letter requesting my support for an airport curfew in Brisbane.

Unofficially I shall have a word where it might help; but officially I am afraid the Federal Government does not interfere in State Government affairs. I am sure you understand.

Yours sincerely, etc.

Dear Mrs . . .

Thank you for pointing out the irritating habit of 'you know'.

It is easy for habits to creep in without one's knowledge, and actually his family have already had a word on the subject!

Yours sincerely, etc.

Dear Mrs . . .

Thank you for your letter and suggestions.

I know the medical benefits issue is one that concerns the Government very much because I have heard them talking about it. The problem is the stupefying cost to the country of free medical care for all, or whether or not to put the onus on people themselves. I know they are trying very hard to sort this one out for the general good of everybody. Anyway, I shall pass your remarks on to Malcolm at some stage.

Yours sincerely, etc.

Dear Mr . . .

Thank you very much for your letter telling me the story of 'Tamie Fraser'. The little filly sounds adorable.

I am most touched to be asked to have the horse named after me, but I feel bearing my name would bring her nothing but bad luck, as the human Tamie Fraser is less than speedy on the ground. I also believe there is some difficulty in naming a horse after a person, when registering with the VRC.

Anyway, when you find her a name, do let me know, and I will watch her progress with interest.

Yours sincerely, etc.

Dear . . .

Your mother and you have obviously had a hard life and coped with it very well When mums and daughters love each other things seem to work out in the end.

I am glad you are happy with your step-father and his son. Perhaps you will soon be old enough to help mum in the shop so she'll be able to sit down.

Yours sincerely, etc.

Dear Mr . . .

I only hope your predictions are not as fatalistic as they sound.

179

Hopefully, despite the fate as told by the stars, the best man will win, and the Prime Minister of 1977 will be there in 1978. I think it is up to the people and not the stars.

Yours sincerely, etc.

Dear . . .

Thank you for your letter drawing my attention to the likelihood of Government legislation to ban the docking of dog's tails.

I had no idea this possibility was in existence. I will certainly try to find out who is involved in the move and lodge your protest with them.

Yours sincerely, etc.

Dear Mrs . . .

I have never heard of your proven laryngitus remedy but I am very pleased you sent it.

If, indeed, the Prime Minister does fall prey to another attack of this kind I will definitely try it out.

Yours sincerely, etc.

Dear Mrs . . .

Thank you for your letter concerning the fluoridation of your water.

I appreciate your arguments against the fluoridation of water in Victoria, and I have passed on your letter to the Department of Health. However, this problem comes under State Government jurisdiction, and I cannot be as effective as if it were a Federal matter.

Yours sincerely, etc.

Dear Mrs . . .

As I am not an expert in the field of Veterans' Affairs, I have asked the Minister, Mr. Adermann, if he would have a look at your situation and see what can be done to help.

Sometimes these things take awhile but don't think you have been forgotten.

Yours sincerely, etc.

Dear Mrs . . .

Thank you for sending the information pamphlet on the Hoboba bean.

It is the first I have heard of it, and when things quieten down after the initial excitement of arriving home, I will sit down and read all about it.

Yours sincerely, etc.

Dear Mrs . . .

I am afraid I find my voice all too namby-pamby for words. But I have taken note of your suggestion about the letter 'i' and will experiment.

Yours sincerely, etc.

Dear Mr . . .

I was most interested to read your views on effective ways of bringing home to the Russians how other nations feel about their invasion of Afghanistan. You have certainly put forward some thought-provoking remarks, and I will pass these on to Mr. Ellicott, the Minister for Home Affairs, who has responsibility for sporting matters.

Yours sincerely, etc.

Dear Mr . . .

The Israeli Army Diet, so-called, was 2 days apples: 2 days cheese; 2 days chicken and 2 days salad taken with water only, no alcohol.

You must return to normal food at the end of this time.

Another good diet which is not quite such torture is the pure protein diet which is meat, cheese or eggs, grilled or boiled but no fats or sauces. Again, 10 glasses of water a day. At least on this one you can eat as much as you like of the pure protein foods. This you can stick to for no longer than three weeks. I hope it is a success.

Yours sincerely, etc.

Dear Mr . . .

I was most impressed by your poem which expressed such sincere patriotism. However, as Australians have now decided on a national anthem, our country has a tune to play on moments of national importance.

Yours sincerely, etc.

Dear Mr . . .

Thank you for your letter concerning your plague of rats.

I have forwarded your letter on to the New South Wales division of the Keep Australia Beautiful Council for their comments and action. I do hope they may be able to help.

Yours sincerely, etc.

Dear Mrs . . .

I am glad you liked my (royal) wedding outfit. Most of my clothes I confess I wear for a very long time until they look pretty limp and tired with all the travelling, and when I do have a clearance I send everything to St. Vincent de Paul.

Yours sincerely, etc.

Dear Mr . . .

I believe that if you want to do something well, or attain your goals in life, you cannot rely on other people's opinions of you to form your own opinion of yourself. Worthwhile things do not come with ease, and I am afraid you must plod along with your goals in sight until you achieve them. This is the meaning of the saying: 'Life wasn't meant to be easy'; that if you want to achieve something, then success is going to take hard work and dedication, whatever field you are in.

Yours sincerely, etc.

Dear Mr . . .

Thank you for the information about the 'drip' method of irrigation.

I shall pass it all on to Malcolm to read as he is more knowledgeable about such things than I.

Yours sincerely, etc.

Dear Mrs . . .

You do seem to be having trouble with your neighbours.

I am sure the big car and dog were not bought with welfare money. Most Asian students have allowances sent to them by their parents.

I am sorry I cannot be any more help, other than to sympathise that where you came to live in your retirement is not as quiet as you had hoped it would be.

Yours sincerely, etc.

Dear Mr . . .

I shall read the article you sent me with much interest.

As you know, decisions for sex education in schools are made independently by state governments without any Commonwealth direction, but thank you anyway for keeping me informed.

Yours sincerely, etc.

Dear Miss . . .

I am asking around about your wish to meet the Queen.

In the meantime I thought I had better write to make sure you didn't think I'd forgotten about the matter.

Yours sincerely, etc.

Dear Mrs . . .

Thank you for your letter and enclosed (newspaper) cutting.

It is always interesting to read the views of clair-voyants to see how much success they have. I was so glad to read that the Prime Minister will be returned at the next election in 1983.

Yours sincerely, etc.

Chapter 22
THE FALL

In politics 'if . . . ' is a futile concept. 'If . . . ' is an inherently barren exercise. 'If . . . ' is a pointless game of self-immolation, and I have *never*, either before or since the ill-fated election of 1983, known the Frasers to indulge in it.

I am not so wise nor so strong, however, and late one night in the aftermath of that election I said to Eda (the other politician in the family and currently the President of the Liberal Party in Victoria), '*If* Bill Hayden had stepped down from the leadership of the Labor party just one hour earlier on February 3, 1983 . . . *if* Malcolm had hung on until October '83 when the drought had broken, the world economic recovery was underway and his wages pause had started to bite . . . *if* his back surgery had not ruled out an early election in December '82 when we won the seat of Flinders . . .'

'And *if* your aunt had balls—she'd be your uncle!' said Eda. Point taken. I didn't dwell on the subject again.

Many and various have been the theories proposed by political analysts as to why the Prime Minister called an election in March, 1983, six months ahead of time. But whatever his reasons, and I'm sure they were urgent and various, at 12.40 pm on February 3, he called on the Governor-General in Canberra and handed over a letter requesting a double dissolution of parliament. In Brisbane just ten minutes later, at 12.40, Bill Hayden stepped down as leader of the Labor Party, clearing the way for Bob Hawke to assume the leadership. At 5.00 pm the Prime Minister announced that the Governor General had assented to his request for an election for both Houses of Parliament. It was arguably the most dramatic day in Australian politics since November 11, 1975.

'I was up in Armidale NSW setting up young Hugh in a cottage on a property where he had been appointed as overseer,' Tam told me. 'I was walking around a supermarket loaded up with mops and buckets and brooms and a little old lady came up to me, and said: "Mrs. Fraser, what is your husband up to?" and I said well, you tell me what he is up to? "He has just called an election!" she said.

'When I found out that not only had Malcolm called an election but that Hawke had superceded Hayden at the same time, my instant reaction was—we're a goner. Because Hawke has a folk hero image in Australia.

'I think things started to go wrong for the government about April, 1982, when Andrew Peacock challenged Malcolm for the leadership. Malcolm never at any stage thought he would lose a vote against Peacock. He knew he had the confidence of the party. But the whole air of public dissention was enough to make the polls rocket downwards. 45 degrees. And Malcolm said to me then, "Dissention is the one thing the electorate will not tolerate in any party. People can't bear public squabbling." He said, "I really think this is going to make it a hell of a battle to win the next election."'

Across Australia the tide of politics was beginning to change. In Tasmania the change was from Labor to Liberal, with the election to office of Robin Gray, but elsewhere it was flowing the other way. In April the Labor Party in Victoria under leader John Cain ended 27 years of unbroken Liberal rule. In November John Bannon and his Labor team defeated the Tonkin Liberal Government in South Australia, and the following February Brian Burke won government for Labor in Western Australia.

Late in 1982 Sir Phillip Lynch retired from politics because of ill-health and a by-election had to be held in his seat of Flinders. Flinders had been a swinging seat before Sir Phillip's careful stewardship had secured it for the Liberal Party, and with him no longer there Labor believed they would win it. Besides, the Prime Minister was flat out on a hospital bed after undergoing surgery on his back, unable to take any part in the campaign.

So Tam went down to Flinders to fight Bill Hayden in support of the Liberal candidate, Peter Reith. 'It was nothing really. All I did was fly the flag, make a few speeches, shake a lot of hands, that sort of thing. It was no big deal.' Maybe not, but when the Liberals emerged victorious after the poll, *The Age* ran a cartoon by Nicholson depicting Tamie in boxing shorts in a boxing ring, gloved hand held high in victory, while at her feet lay the inert figure of Bill Hayden, out for the count.

Malcolm's stay in hospital cost him the option of an early election, but I remember my mother remarking one day after she had been to visit him that he had told her every Prime Minister should undergo surgery at least once a year—to force them into taking a rest. He said the day-to-day demands of office are so constant and so overwhelming that a PM never gets the chance to step back, to stand apart from issues, and weigh them at a distance; there is never enough time to ponder.

'Malcolm worked out the wages freeze when he was in hospital, and how to get the unions to agree to it,' Tam said. 'Part of the agreement was that the Government money saved on wages was going to be spent on capital works to create more jobs. And that was the thing that made it palatable, why people were prepared to buy it. Because if you were rejecting the wage freeze, quite clearly you would be rejecting more jobs. The wages freeze was a great success which Labor subsequently inherited. Malcolm thought it through sitting up in hospital, although Tam found him one day watching *Yes, Minister* on the TV with Geoff Yeend, his department head, and Doug Anthony— and all of them laughing in different places!'

To the accompaniment of the 1983 Liberal theme song, 'We're not waiting for the world!' Malcolm launched the party's election campaign on February 15, promising no tax cuts, but a package of $568 million in various targeted areas and tough new industrial laws. The next night Bob Hawke promised to Bring Australia Together, pledging tax cuts, higher welfare benefits, job schemes and capital works. This was Ash Wednesday and on that afternoon 72 people lost their lives and over 2000 homes were destroyed in many separate bushfires which raged across Victoria and South Australia. Next morning, with the nation in shock, both sides by mutual consent called a halt to the campaign, and Tam and the PM set off to tour the devastated areas.

For the Liberals, the campaign never really regained its momentum. As Tam said: 'You know when you are winning or losing. It becomes apparent from the way things are reported; things become more negative. One incident that helped me to know we were on the skids was when the kids went to see Barry Humphries one night. In his show he sent up Malcolm in the usual way, and everyone laughed and enjoyed it; then he sent up Hawke and he couldn't get a laugh when he was sending up Hawke. Hawke somehow wasn't to be laughed at. So he dropped the subject like a hot cake and when the kids came home and told me about it I thought well, we're gone.'

The opinion polls were confirming Tamie's judgement. Bob Hawke, aware of a nagging doubt in the electorate about his basic stability, campaigned coolly, almost managing to be dull. It was a most effective tactic.

Meanwhile Malcolm crossed and re-crossed the nation in a desperate attempt to point out what he saw as the danger of Labor's policies. Tamie was constantly with him. 'The Liberal Party always tried to get me to campaign on my own, to be a separate identity, and it was something I always resisted. At each election they'd say now you do these things and the PM will do those. But Malcolm and I discussed it and what we really wanted to do was work together, to present a family sort of entity. You see, I never felt demeaned by just tagging along with Malcolm; I didn't ever feel that I needed to identify myself by doing my own thing in politics and campaign separately. Politics was his game, his career, not mine. I was only part of it through being married to him, and I never wanted to pretend anything else.'

On February 19 in a state election held in Western Australia Labor won office with a massive swing of 8%. It was the fall of the last mainland state Liberal Government, and devastating news for the coalition.

But a few days later they received a leaked copy of Labor's prices and incomes policy which caused a brief flurry of excitement, I remember. Malcolm called it 'in every sense a blueprint for union government; it means government by the unions for the unions.' He said it would lock the economy into an inflationary spiral and thought the people would reject it out of hand.

Instead, the people saw it as a recipe for industrial peace.

Then in response to remarks by Paul Keating about using Australian bank holdings to finance the government deficit, Malcolm said Labor would be robbing the savings of the people. He said that under Labor people's savings would be safer under the bed. The remarks caused an uproar, but considering what's happened to the dollar since . . .

One day towards the end of the campaign Tam called in briefly to see Eda in Melbourne. Her face looked white and pinched. Tamie has a small face anyway, and this day it seemed minute. 'I think we're in real trouble,' she told Eda. 'I think we're going to lose. And what I'm really scared about is not losing, but what's going to happen to this country if Labor gets in.'

But out on the hustings it was Smile! Smile! Smile! *Never* show a doubt. *Never* give an inch. *Never* give up hope. Optimism was her armour and she showed not the slightest chink. 'Of course we're going to win!' she told a TV audience in Brisbane. 'Yes, completely confident!' she declared brightly in a radio interview in Sydney. 'Oh, I dare say Malcolm may retire when he's 80!' she conceded with a laugh to a newspaper reporter in Hobart.

The opinion polls continued their downward slide.

Election night on March 3 came all too soon. Again, to our eternal regret, Chris and I were unable to be there. But Phoebe told me about it.

'Well, Arma (her Fraser Grandmother) arranged dinner for us at her flat in South Yarra' she said. 'There were about 20 people, I guess. The family, all except for Hugh who was up at Armidale, and some old friends. The atmosphere was pretty quiet and tense. I mean, everyone was being cheerful, but it was a kind of forced cheerfulness. It felt like when someone is having an operation in hospital and you are sitting there waiting for the result and trying to be brave and wondering whether it's going to be alright; that sort of sick feeling at the pit of your stomach when you really don't know what the result will be; you're afraid it might be pretty bad but you keep desperately hoping it won't be. I mean, despite what the polls said, we really didn't know what would happen and everyone kept hoping against hope.

'Mum was constantly rushing around looking after people, making sure they were okay, keeping their spirits up—and all the while keeping a close eye on Dad. Dad never took his eyes off the TV.'

A positive trend was painfully slow in appearing. Most political pundits had thought a result would be apparent early, but 9pm came and went and although a swing was showing, would it be across the board or confined only to Labor's safe seats? Conversely, would it show only in seats held safely by Liberals where a protest vote for Hawke would not affect the outcome? And what of Western Australia, two hours behind in the count?

The night wore on. The family watched and waited. Hope slowly bled away.

By eleven-thirty a Labor win seemed inevitable. 'No!' said Malcolm. 'The West will save us! The West will come in for us!'

The West did not come in for us.

'Eventually we all realised it was curtains,' Phoebe said. 'I think Dad knew all along in his heart of hearts, but he was putting on a brave face. It's funny, but what really impressed me about Dad that night was that he really wasn't sad for himself, he was just sorry that it should happen when everything was starting to look up, despite the fires and the drought and that awful year before.

'I think he felt that he'd done the hard part and now everything was going to be thrown away. I mean any-one with two ears and a brain in their head could work out what would happen if the Labor Party kept their election promises which were to cut taxes and increase spending. Dad said, "I bloody-well hope they don't keep them, because if they do it will be a disaster for this country."

'Just after midnight we all went in to the Southern Cross Hotel. There was a big crowd outside and we had to push our way through them to get in, but it wasn't as bad as when we were leaving. That was really horrible. A huge mob of people screaming and jostling and jeering at us. And it was so pointless! I mean, we'd lost! We were gone! It was as though they not only wanted to see us fall, but to kick us in the head as well.

'But when we got inside the hotel all the staff were there waiting and it was so warming to see them, plus the friends who had come in to be with us. And I remember mum saying how terribly much it meant to her that people had stayed on and on that night waiting, even when it was obvious we'd lost, to say "Hi!" and "Stiff luck, old chaps!" and sort of stick beside you. That's the kind of thing you never forget, the people that stay with you when things are bad.

'We were in those private function rooms upstairs which the Liberal Party always has on election nights—

190

and there was the same sort of setup as usual with food and drink and a band playing. But no-one felt like dancing. At one stage we were just milling around and Colleen Hewett, the singer who had recorded the Liberal Party campaign song, came up to me, and said: 'Phoebe, I am telling you this because I thought you would like to know. When I began this campaign, I wasn't political, it was just a job. I wasn't voting for your Dad. That's the way it was. But as I've travelled around the country with him and heard what he is saying, and really listened to what he was saying, and got to know him, for the first time in my life I felt really safe.'' She said, ''Your Mum and Dad are such warm people and being with them just made me feel everything will be OK.'''

Finally the numbers were irrefutable—the Labor Party had won a great victory, a two-party preferred swing of 4% and 25 seats in the House of Representatives. 'Just after one o'clock, I think it was, Dad went out to concede,' Phoebe went on. 'He and Mum slipped away before we were aware, and we had to push through the crowd to catch up to them. We found a funny little tin platform to stand on so that we could see over people's heads. There were already about eight people on it and when Angela and I got on as well it collapsed bang! crash! We were in tears of laughter and tears of pain and so we really didn't hear what Dad was saying, but apparently he was pretty upset. And as Angela said later, I don't know whether we were robbed of sharing that experience— or spared from it.'

I was not spared from it. Back at Balmoral, clinging on to Chris's hand, I watched it all on TV, the tears streaming down my face. 'Ladies and Gentlemen, I have a short statement that I would like to make,' Malcolm began, coming forward into the full glare of the lights. Tamie was at his side. 'Firstly, I would like to congratulate Mr. Hawke and the Australian Labor Party for winning this election. I hope they can achieve what they intend for the people of Australia. They have set a high ambition and I hope they can achieve it because if they can it will advantage this country.' His words came slowly and deliberately and his features wore everything he'd ever had to face as Australia's second-longest serving Prime Minister. 'I want to say that from this moment I resign from the leadership of the Liberal Party. I will not contest the leadership of the Liberal Party . . . I want to make it plain that I take full responsibility for the timing of the Federal election. I take total responsibility for the conduct of that election; I therefore take total responsibility for the defeat of the Liberal Party.' It was too much. He paused, and caught his breath. Tamie, ever strong, reached out for his hand. Steadied, he continued: 'I would like to thank all my colleagues and the Liberal Party right around Australia for the support they have given me, not just over recent weeks, but for the past seven years.' Then Peter Harvey from Channel 9 asked: 'Mr. Fraser, do you also intend to resign from parliament?'

'Oh, I think that, Peter, can wait for a day or two,' Malcolm replied. 'There really has been magnificent support in very difficult times. There are many wonderful people who believed in what the Government was doing and I thank them for that.' So saying he turned away to where Mark, his eldest son, beside him at the first election, was waiting there to be beside him at the last. Again there was no need for words between them.

As I watched Tam turned from the cameras, too, and made her way back through the crowd to her family. Gently she gathered them together and guided them away, out of the room, out of the hotel and out of political life.

The show was over.